D1025349

18 DAYS IN TAHRIR: STORIES FROM EGYPT'S REVOLUTION

Published in Hong Kong by Haven Books Limited
www.havenbooksonline.com

ISBN 978-988-19195-8-8

18 DAYS IN TAHRIR

STORIES FROM EGYPT'S REVOLUTION

HATEM RUSHDY, EDITOR

HAVEN BOOKS | Publishing

For the martyrs

CONTENTS

FOREWORD:
NEWBORN REVOLUTION

Ahdaf Soueif

I have friends on anti-depressants who, over the last twenty days, forgot to take their pills and have now thrown them away. Such is the effect of the Egyptian Revolution.

On Friday night, Egypt partied. Chants and songs and drums and joy-cries rang out from Alexandria to Aswan. The defunct regime was only mentioned in reference to "we want our money back".

Otherwise, three chants were dominant, and very telling: One —"Lift your head up high, you're Egyptian"—was a response to how humiliated, how hopeless we'd been made to feel over the last four decades.

The second was: "We'll get married, we'll have kids," and reflected the hopes of the millions whose desperate need for jobs and homes had been driving them to risk their lives to illegally cross the sea to Europe or the desert to Libya.

The third chant was: "Everyone who loves Egypt, come and rebuild Egypt."

And on Saturday, they were as good as their word: they came and cleaned up after their revolution.

Volunteers who arrived in Tahrir [Square] after mid-day found it spick and span, and started cleaning up other streets instead. I saw kids perched on the great lions of Qasr el-Nil Bridge, buffing them up.

I feel—and every parent will know what I mean—I feel that I

need to keep my concentration trained on this baby, this newborn revolution. I need to hold it safe in my mind and my heart every second, until it grows and steadies a bit. Eighty million of us feel this way right now.

Eighty million at least—because the support we've been getting from the world has been phenomenal. There's been something different, something very special, about the quality of the attention the Egyptian revolution has attracted: it's been... personal.

People everywhere have taken what's been happening here personally. And they've let us know. And those direct, positive and emotional messages we've been receiving have put the wind in our sails.

We have a lot to learn very quickly. But we're working.

And the people, everywhere, are with us.

Cairo
February 13th, 2011

INTRODUCTION

Millions turned out in the tumultuous 18 days from late January to mid-February 2011, which led to the fall of Hosni Mubarak, president of Egypt for nearly 30 years. While there had been earlier protests and Internet campaigns, none of those who turned out in Tahrir Square on January 25th could have predicted that Mubarak would be finally ousted. It was a campaign generated by ordinary people, but its impetus came from opposition groups, the death of a young man in Alexandria and partially the efforts of a Google executive who became one of the key heroes of the Egyptian revolution.

Wael Ghonim founded a Facebook page called "We are all Khaled Said", in reference to a young man who had been arrested and beaten to death by policemen in Alexandria the previous year, causing widespread public anger. Ghonim's Facebook campaign called for people to protest at different venues and was quickly shut down by the government.

But Ghonim's use of the Internet to call the people out, with parallel calls by other groups, brought about a revolution that used Facebook, Twitter, BlackBerry messages and other electronic technologies to create a public movement of millions of people. Ghonim was detained for 12 days during the revolution, and all of that time he was blindfolded. While he kindly provided this book with the use of his slogan, he is now preparing to publish his own book and has taken a sabbatical from his job as Google's head of marketing in the Middle East and North Africa.

"I call this Revolution 2.0," Ghonim said in an interview with

American current affairs program *60 Minutes*. "I say that our revolution is like Wikipedia: everyone is contributing content. You don't know the names of the people contributing the content. This is exactly what happened. Revolution 2.0 in Egypt was exactly the same."

Well, in this book, we name some of those who provided the content. Our contributors are largely ordinary Egyptians: young, old, wealthy and not so well-off, Muslim, Christian, men and women, some of whom had demonstrated before and many who hadn't. The housewife and mother, who suddenly found herself Googling the best methods to stave off the effects of tear gas and creating kits to give out to fellow protesters. Then there were those who became adept at making Molotov cocktails and grabbing anything that would constitute a weapon to protect their neighborhoods after 30,000 convicts flooded the streets a few days into the revolution.

For those reading this book in a liberal democracy, where you can stand in the street and openly criticize the government, or call the country's leader a fool or worse, with no fear of arrest or torture, protesting in Egypt is on a whole different level. During those 18 days, protesters had to contend with real, hardcore violence, choking and vomiting from the effects of tear gas, being shot at with both rubber bullets and live ammunition, and—with snipers stationed on rooftops—never quite knowing where those bullets might come from. The official death toll for the Egyptian revolution is more than 300 but hundreds more disappeared. Then there are the several thousand who survived, many left with severe head injuries from the stones that rained down on them.

Plenty of historical and academic accounts are now emerging of the revolution, and will continue to do so, especially as time allows for more perspective on January and February's events in Egypt's current and future political context. But this book is confined to just those 18 days: what those individuals sharing their stories thought of the unfolding demonstrations on a daily basis, what they saw, conversations they had with protesters who had joined from all over Egypt, and what they suffered in that time. It is remarkable to read how some citizens, whose lives were distinctly comfortable under Mubarak's rule in comparison with some of their compatriots, were quite prepared to die in Tahrir Square. That was how strongly they felt.

As this book prepares to go to print, Egypt is undergoing tremendous change. The elation and jubilation that accompanied Mubarak's exit has dissipated to a certain extent. While the army was always held in high esteem, its behaviour towards demonstrators in more recent months—including beatings and torture—resulted in its reputation being held in lower esteem than before. Protesters kissed soldiers during the revolution, grateful that the army did not use their guns on the people. Now time will tell as to whether the Higher Military Council will stand by its earlier guarantees to provide security while allowing room for civilian-rule elections to take place .

But, for now, let us return to those days in January and February when even poets, singers and artists joined those in Tahrir Square amid the violence and destruction. In transcribing protesters' accounts for this book, we relayed their stories as much as possible as they had told them in their own words and in their own style, to capture the immediacy of thoughts and emotion.

We reserved the concluding segment of each account for the chapter entitled "The Moment He Quit", to show the people's reactions during those palpable moments when they each realized the revolution had achieved its primary aim.

Egyptians at Tahrir Square struggled with exhaustion, fear, uncertainty—but ultimately they have a story to tell of hope for their future.

Sign on baby: "Leave! Grandad and Daddy were quite enough for you."

ارحل
كفاية طلبناك
جدو وبابا

Photo: Azza Tawfik

TIMELINE OF
THE REVOLUTION

2010

FRIDAY, DECEMBER 17ᵀᴴ
Tarek Mohamed Bouazizi, a Tunisian street vendor, sets himself on fire, after being harassed and humiliated by a bribe-seeking municipal officer.

2011

MONDAY, JANUARY 17ᵀᴴ
Abdou Abdul Moneim, an Egyptian food-stand owner and father of four, sets himself on fire in front of Parliament after a failed argument with municipal officers over his monthly coupons for subsidized bread. Over the next week, there are three more attempts at self-immolation.

TUESDAY, JANUARY 18ᵀᴴ
Egyptian Foreign Minister, Ahmed Aboul Gheit, says: "The talk about the spread of what happened in Tunisia to Egypt is nonsense. Each society has its own circumstances … if the Tunisian people decide to take that approach, [that's] their business." Egypt said the Tunisian people's will is what counts.

MONDAY, JANUARY 24ᵀᴴ
Minister of Interior, Habib el-Adly, says: "Setting yourself on fire is immature and will achieve nothing."

TUESDAY, JANUARY 25TH

Day of Revolt. Protesters in several Egyptian cities, including Cairo, Alexandria and Suez, clash with riot police during demonstrations caused by rising frustration with the police state, poverty, rising prices and lack of political freedoms. Protesters use Facebook, Twitter and other social media to communicate.

In Cairo, thousands are beaten and tear-gassed at midnight to stop them spending the night in the square. Some 500 demonstrators are arrested. Police boast that the square was emptied in less than half an hour. The government blames the Muslim Brotherhood for inciting the protests.

WEDNESDAY, JANUARY 26TH

Protests continue after news that three people were killed the previous day. Suez is a major clashing point, with 55 protesters and more than 10 police officers seriously injured.

THURSDAY, JANUARY 27TH

The government instructs mobile-phone operators and Internet service providers to stop BlackBerry Messenger, Twitter and Facebook services. The rest of the Internet is still accessible. Demonstrations continue in several cities. Cairo, Suez, Alexandria, Tanta and Ismailiya all witness violent clashes between demonstrators and police forces.

Text messages and What's App messages go out in the evening listing some 35 mosques and churches as meeting points for demonstrations to start from on what is being called Friday of Rage. Minister of Interior Habib el-Adly warns that the police will use decisive measures to dispel any demonstrations.

FRIDAY, JANUARY 28TH

Friday of Rage. The government cuts off Internet and text messaging. Users report that text messages appear to be sent but do not arrive at the recipient's end.

Thousands gather at churches and mosques all over Egypt following Friday midday prayers. Chants of "The people want to overthrow the regime" and "Down with Hosni Mubarak" are heard all over Cairo and other cities. Across Egypt, demonstrators and Central Security forces clash. In Cairo, tens of thousands converge on Tahrir; police use tear gas, water cannons, batons and, in some cases, rubber bullets to try to disperse demonstrations. But they are unsuccessful. Many injuries, some severe, are reported in Cairo, but no deaths.

The city of Suez reports more than 10 demonstrators and one policeman have been killed in clashes. Army troops are deployed but retain a neutral stance.

Late in the night, the Egyptian president speaks on state television. He announces he is firing his prime minister and the government, but shows no sign of leaving power.

Tens of thousands in Cairo reach Tahrir Square after violent clashes with police. Most spend the night in the square. Demonstrators set fire to the National Democratic Party Headquarters close to Tahrir and right next door to the Egyptian Museum of Antiquities, home to the largest collection of Pharaonic artefacts including the famed Tutankhamen mask. The army moves to protect the museum from looting.

Police are withdrawn from the streets as prisons across the country are torched. As thousands of inmates are released on to the streets, rumors spread amid fears of looting and rampaging.

SATURDAY, JANUARY 29TH
For the first time in 30 years, Mubarak appoints a vice-president, General Intelligence Chief Omar Suleiman, a close friend and confidante of Mubarak's. Rumors on the street are that Mubarak has left the country, some say to Abu Dhabi, others Saudi Arabia, others say he is still in the country, but has left for the resort of Sharm el Sheikh. This last rumor is strengthened by information that the army has deployed significant troops in the southern Sinai resort.

Tahrir Square remains a tense area, with tens of thousands of demonstrators setting up tents and clashing periodically with police. All mobile-phone communication has been switched off and Internet services remain down. There is no police presence at all on the streets of Cairo. Neighborhood watches are organized with residents of each neighborhood manning makeshift stations in their districts. They arm themselves with sticks, knives and, in some cases, guns to prevent burglary and other crime.

A curfew is declared and generally ignored.

SUNDAY, JANUARY 30TH

The US Embassy in Cairo urges all American passport-holders to leave the country immediately. Turkey sends aircraft to evacuate its citizens. Mohamed ElBaradei, Egyptian Nobel Peace Prize winner and ex-Chief of the International Atomic Energy Agency (IAEA) speaks to the crowds in Tahrir, stating that what has been started by them cannot be undone, urging steadfastness and resilience in the face of what he expects will be a tough battle with the regime.

MONDAY, JANUARY 31ST

Apparently still supporting Mubarak's position, the US advises the Egyptian president to respond to his people's wishes for increased freedoms. More than a quarter of a million people are now permanently camped out in Tahrir Square. Chants have changed from "The People Demand the Regime's Fall!" to "The People Demand the President's Departure!" The army reassures the demonstrators in Tahrir Square, declaring clearly that it will never "aim its weapons at Egyptian chests". Strengthened by this guarantee, protesters call for a million-man march on the following day.

A new cabinet is formed by Mubarak, with mostly minor changes, but with one significant alteration: the much-hated Minister of Interior Habib el-Adly, known on Cairo streets as Minister of Torture, is replaced by Mahmoud Wagdi, a lesser-known figure.

Israel—a country that once described Mubarak as a strategic treasure—demands that world governments minimize pressure on him to leave, citing the need for stability in the region.

TUESDAY, FEBRUARY 1ST

Close to a million people gather in Tahrir. What started as a middle-class demonstration has turned into a full-fledged revolutionary movement comprising all segments of Egyptian society. Wealthy and poor, Muslims and Christians, illiterates and intelligentsia all swarm to the square, demanding Mubarak's departure.

In his second speech to the people since the start of the unrest, Mubarak announces that he will not, and was never planning to, run in the next presidential elections. In what is seen by many as a move to gain the emotional support of sentimental Egyptians, Mubarak says he is a patriot who wishes to die in his country, a military man who has put his life on the line in wars for Egypt. In the same speech and in a thinly veiled threat, and perhaps as a word of warning to the international community as well, he says the choice now is between stability and chaos. He also promises changes to the infamous Article 76, recently re-engineered to make it all but impossible for non-National Democratic Party (NDP) members to run for the presidency. The joke around Cairo was that this article was originally worded "You cannot run for President unless your name is Gamal Mubarak and your father is the current president of Egypt".

People on the street are divided between allowing Mubarak to leave in dignity and insisting he leave immediately.

In what seems like a 180-degree turn, President Obama withdraws earlier support for Mubarak, saying only the people of Egypt can choose their leader.

Although Tahrir Square is now the revolution's focal point, tens of thousands of demonstrators are filling all central areas of major Egyptian cities. Train services to Cairo and underground metro services to Tahrir are stopped.

New Prime Minister Ahmed Shafik says he guarantees with his life the security of the protesters in Tahrir.

WEDNESDAY, FEBRUARY 2ND

Day of the Camel. After Mubarak's sentimental speech, many leave Tahrir, but many others remain, not believing his promises. Rumors abound of a pro-Mubarak demonstration marching towards Tahrir. At around noon, several thousand pro-Mubarak protesters attack the square. In an eerily medieval scene, scores of hired thugs rush in on camel-back, others on horseback, armed with knives, swords and whips. An ensuing battle, since dubbed The Battle of the Camel, lasts well into the small hours of the following morning. During the night, Molotov cocktails and live ammunition are used against the Tahrir protesters. Anti-Mubarak protesters succeed in repelling the attackers and securing the square. Scores are dead and more than a thousand are injured.

All observers conclude that the Muslim Brotherhood was instrumental in repelling the attack by pro-Mubarak demonstrators. Reports from various sources put the number of deaths that day at anywhere between 11 (Egyptian Ministry of Health's estimate) and 150 (international news agencies' estimate).

Internet services are partially restored.

THURSDAY, FEBRUARY 3RD

A group of demonstrators attempting to storm the Ministry of Interior report snipers on the roofs shooting them down, aiming for the head and neck.

Tahrir Square is completely secured by the pro-democracy demonstrators. Checkpoints are set up at all of the square's entrances, where those manning them search people for weapons and arrest any policemen, before handing them over to the army.

Word on the street is that NDP leaders ordered the previous day's attacks.

Another million-man demonstration is announced for the next day, named Departure Friday.

FRIDAY, FEBRUARY 4TH

More than a million people are in Tahrir, but the scene is carnival-like, with singers and street vendors selling everything from food and water to cigarettes, flags and mobile-phone recharge cards. Several Friday prayer sermons are given over loudspeakers and makeshift stages are set up across the square.

SATURDAY, FEBRUARY 5TH

Egyptian state television claims that the people in Tahrir are being controlled by foreign powers.

A gas pipe that supplies Israel with Egyptian natural gas at below international prices (the subject of much anger by Egyptians), is blown up. State television points the finger at terrorists.

Leaders of Mubarak's National Democratic Party resign, including Gamal Mubarak, the president's son and heir apparent.

SUNDAY, FEBRUARY 6TH
Sunday mass is held in Tahrir Square, attended by both Christians and Muslims. After ten days of complete closure, banks open for reduced hours, allowing people and companies to withdraw limited amounts of money. Small numbers of traffic police reappear on Cairo's streets.

MONDAY, FEBRUARY 7TH
Prime Minister Shafik's government announces a 15 per cent increase in all government employees' wages, further signalling how out of touch they are with the people's demands for Mubarak's departure.

Hundreds of thousands continue to camp in Tahrir as protests enter their 12th day.

TUESDAY, FEBRUARY 8TH
Protesters move towards the parliament building and block the government headquarters, forcing the government to hold its meetings at a remote location near the Cairo-Alexandria desert road.

VP Suleiman warns that the government will not accept the continued disruption of life in Egypt for long.

WEDNESDAY, FEBRUARY 9TH
More segments of Egyptian society join the protests, including labor unions. Foreign Minister Aboul Gheit criticises the US stance on the demonstrations, expressing the need for support from the US for the failing government, which has long been a close US ally.

In the first sign of capitulation, the government—through its criminal court—announces the freezing of assets of three former ministers and banning them from travel. At the same time, the Muslim Brotherhood announces that it will not field a candidate for president, in a bid to allay fears that they are hijacking the revolution.

THURSDAY, FEBRUARY 10TH

Scores are killed in protests in El-Wadi el-Gedeed governorate. The prime minister immediately sacks the head of security in the governorate, saying the government guarantees the right of people to protest peacefully.

The army announces that the president will give a speech shortly that will "delight the people and respond fully to their demands". Cautious happiness spreads across the square as everyone anticipates Mubarak will resign.

In defiance of the people's will, the army's announcement and CIA predictions of his imminent departure, Mubarak makes a hugely disappointing speech. The heavily edited address reiterates his decision to stay in power until September's presidential elections to ensure smooth transition of power. He claims the decision is to repudiate international pressure.

The square reacts with fury, shoes are raised in the air, and there are chants of "Those Who Love Egypt, March to the Palace Now!" urging the crowds to march to the presidential palace to pressure the president further. Around 3,000 people march towards the palace, some 100 of them volunteering to man the front lines, effectively offering their lives, in case the army or republican guard decide to fire at them.

FRIDAY, FEBRUARY 11TH

Friday of Departure. 4pm, after thousands had tried to storm the State Television building and thousands more had marched to the Palace, VP Omar Suleiman announces that President Hosni Mubarak has resigned as president and has handed power over to the High Council of Armed Forces.

Millions across Egypt rejoice.

SATURDAY, FEBRUARY 12TH

Day of Cleansing. In a first in revolutionary history, tens of thousands of demonstrators start the first day of a Mubarak-free Egypt by cleaning Tahrir Square.

MAP OF
CENTRAL CAIRO

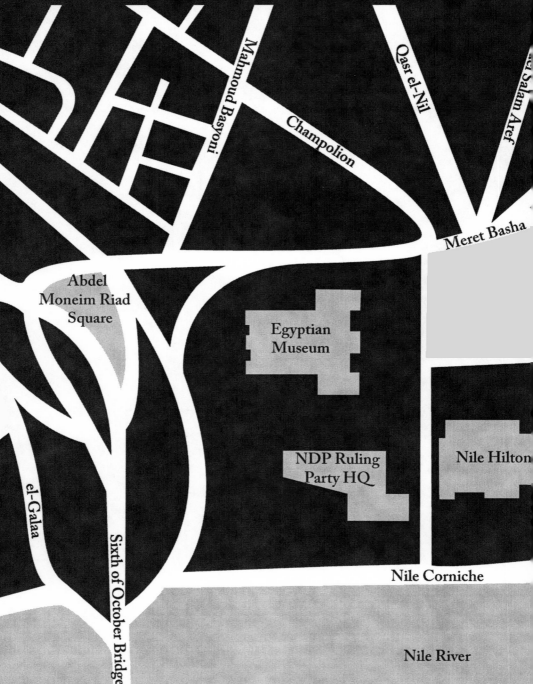

Map of Central Cairo

Mahmoud Basyoni

Champolion

Qasr el-Nil

el Salam Aref

Meret Basha

Abdel
Moneim Riad
Square

Egyptian
Museum

NDP Ruling
Party HQ

Nile Hilton

el-Galaa

Sixth of October Bridge

Nile Corniche

Nile River

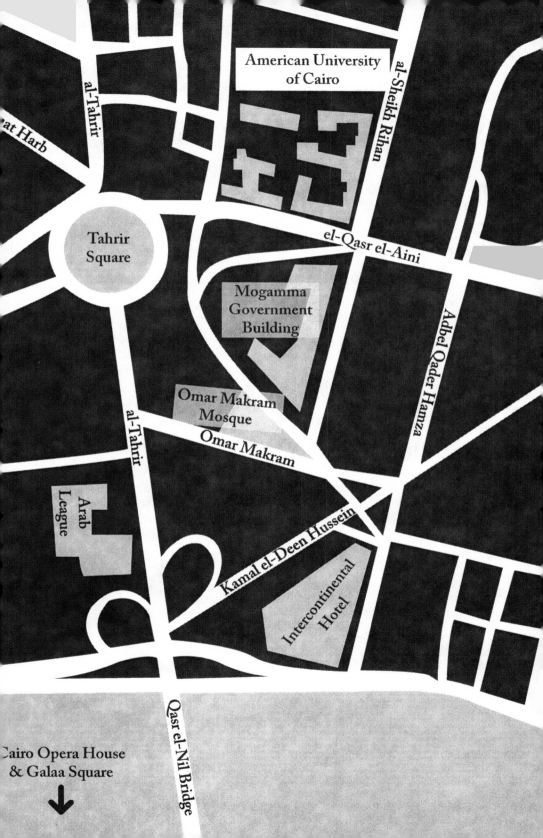

40. Ronald Reagan 1981   1981

41. George H. W. Bush   1989

42. Bill Clinton 1993-2001   1993

43. George W. Bush 2001-2009   2001

44 Barack Obama   2009

Mubarak outlasted four US presidents and the election of the fifth

THREE NEW FACES OF REVOLUTION

Hatem Rushdy

This book is about the 18 days of Egypt's remarkable revolution. It is a collection of stories and experiences that ordinary Egyptians lived through during this unique period. In collecting these stories, I and others spoke with students, professionals, business people, political activists, workers, police officers, an actor who had worked with George Clooney, a former host of *The Islamic Show* which aired in the United States, a film director and two police officers. The stories are told as we heard them.

Through their eyes, I hope this book will document in the most personal way the experiences of a wide spectrum of ordinary and extraordinary Egyptians who made this revolution possible. Just two weeks before it happened, nothing that any of these people dreamed of mattered to the regime.

Such a short time later and for the first time in 30 years, I woke up on Saturday, February 12th, and Hosni Mubarak was *not* the president of my country.

~

I have three short stories of my own, which to me reflect three of the main characteristics of this revolution.

First, it was a peaceful, non-violent cry for freedom. From the first day, cries of "Selmeya!" (Peaceful!) interjected the most famous of our slogans, "Al-Shaab Yureed Eskat el-Nezam!" (The People Want to Topple the Regime!). Second, it is clear that this revolution was a handing over from the old to the new. The use of social media on the Internet—including Facebook and, when the government blocked mobile text messaging, What's App—made this a revolution of the new against a regime in which the average age of leaders was over 70. Third, this was every Egyptian's revolution. Muslims and Christians, men and women, lower, middle and upper classes were all represented in abundance. Demonstrators came to Cairo from every corner of the country to join in Friday of Rage. Muslims kept watch as Sunday mass took place for the Christian martyrs of the revolution. Christians, in turn, formed a protective ring around Muslims as they performed their Friday prayers under the menacing watch of members of the State Security Investigations Service.

My first story took place on Friday, February 4th, the now famous Gomet al-Ghadab or Friday of Rage. My 16-year-old son, Ziyad, and I went for Friday prayers at Mustafa Mahmoud Mosque, one of more than 30 mosques and churches designated as meeting points for the demonstrations. On our way to the mosque, two large trucks belonging to the Central Security Forces passed us; they were filled with paramilitaries in riot-control gear, with helmets, long wooden sticks and shields. Ziyad and I arrived at the mosque and found thousands of people standing in the surrounding streets, listening to the service. The imam gave a very balanced speech. While he agreed that people deserved to have their ambitions met, they also needed strong leadership, he said. When the call for prayer was raised, several hundred people dispersed. It turned out they were Christian, and were clearing the way for the Muslims to pray. They formed a protective human shield between the worshippers and the police forces. After prayers, a cry was raised: "Al-Shaab Yureed Eskat el-Nezam!" (The People Want to Topple the Regime!) and we all started repeating it. The energy was amazing. With voices that loud, surely we would be heard.

We started walking toward Tahrir Square. All the way to Qasr el-Nil Bridge, riot police stood by and just watched us; they kept up with the crowds but did not interfere in any way. At the foot of the bridge, three large riot-control vehicles were poised with water cannons, ready to stop us from crossing the bridge and getting to Tahrir Square. They fired tear gas at us. The stuff really hurts your eyes and nose for about three minutes, but my wife had looked up on the Internet how to deal with it and found that sniffing vinegar or onions relieves the pain in your nostrils, and that soda drinks can ease the sting in your eyes. Ziyad and I were well prepared with little towels soaked in vinegar, but it still hurt badly. It felt as though ten thousand ants were under our skin, trying to eat their way out. Our eyes burned from the inside out and we could not open them. But as Ziyad said, "It doesn't last very long." (Like all instruments of oppression, I add philosophically.) After 20 minutes of our rushing the riot-control police and then retreating under tear-gas attacks, they seemed to run out of canisters and we were finally able to break through the first barricade and get onto the bridge.

And this is the main point of my first story. After getting through that barricade, we found half a dozen security officers and maybe two dozen policemen standing and sitting, exhausted, on the side of the road. These people had fired tear gas at us, viciously beaten the front line of demonstrators with wooden clubs, driven their trucks perilously close to the demonstrators, threatening to run over anyone who dared move forward. Yet, we did not attack them.

There must have been, by this time, easily ten thousand demonstrators to the three dozen policemen and security officers. We could have comfortably beaten them up or worse. But not a single hand was raised against them, not a stone was thrown, not even an insult hurled in their direction. Instead, the cries remained: "Selmeya!". In fact, many of the demonstrators urged them to join us in our march towards Tahrir, an invitation they all refused. This peacefulness, this non-belligerence, this insistence on non-violence even in the face of brutality, was to be a hallmark of our revolution.

My second story happened on the morning of Friday, February 11ᵗʰ, the day that Omar Suleiman would announce Mubarak's relinquishing of his post as President of the Arab Republic of Egypt. The previous night, Mubarak had made his infamous "not going anywhere" speech to the people, confounding everyone including US President Barack Obama. For about half an hour after that speech, Tahrir had gone silent; people were in tears, some had fainted in disbelief. My wife had chest pains; I was numb with anger and disbelief. But on the following morning, Friday the 11th, a "march of ten million" was planned. Everyone from everywhere was in Tahrir, it seemed, and so we manned the entrances with extra vigilance. Since February 2nd, the notorious Day of the Camel, we had barricaded all the entrances to the square, refusing entrance to anyone working for the Ministry of Interior or belonging to the ruling National Democratic Party. We would check people's IDs and then frisk them for any weapons. Over the days, we caught people bringing knives, lead pipes and even a gun or two, and we found many trying to get in who were police officers. They were all handed over to the army officers present in Tahrir.

As I stood at one of the entrances, an old man was walking into Tahrir; he was over 70. He came over to me, showed me his ID and raised his arms to allow me to pat him down. I apologized to him and smiled, explaining that it was a necessary precaution, that we had caught some thugs and some weapons. Suddenly as I finished checking him, he hugged me tight and started crying. "I am sorry, I am so sorry my son," he said. "I am so sorry we left you the country in this state. I am sorry we didn't do anything to stop this bastard earlier." He held me for a full two or three minutes, crying freely over my shoulder, apologizing for his generation's shortcomings. "We were cowardly and weak; nobody dared open his mouth with a word of dissent. We had no Internet to communicate, we had no Facebook. I don't even have a computer. Please," he went on, "teach your children about this revolution, teach them to never give up their rights, you are the future, you and your children, this country's future is in your hands. Don't let the government fool you, please, teach your children to use computers and to use the Internet. Please, teach them to use Facebook, you can teach a lot of people on the Internet, I am sure of it."

When he had calmed down, I held him close. I was in tears myself. I believed it was true; this was a revolution by the new over the old. We had broadcast our messages on BlackBerrys and via What's App. We had communicated online, and the majority of the demonstrators (especially during the first few days) were young people of both genders. It was no longer feasible for Mubarak to keep his people in the dark. The Internet, satellite television, mobile phones, all of these meant that whatever happened anywhere in Egypt became known in the rest of Egypt and indeed the rest of the world, instantly. No more media blackouts, no more cutting off the communication—in with the new!

My third story took place on the morning of Saturday, February 12th. This was Day 19; Mubarak had abdicated the day before. Responding to a Facebook message to come down to Tahrir to clean up, my wife and I headed there armed with brooms, surgical gloves and about a thousand garbage bags. We chose a street that had fewer people cleaning it than on the square itself and started sweeping and collecting garbage in the bags. We had about a hundred surgical gloves, so we distributed these as well. We finished cleaning the side street we were on and went into the square itself.

It was a beautiful sight. Crowds of teenagers were sitting on their knees by the sidewalks painting them in alternating black and white. Some people were trying to cross the sidewalk while the paint was still wet and so we started organizing a line of people along the sidewalk to prevent people from going on to it.

As we guarded the wet paint, a young man of about 30 came over and started talking to me. He was elated, euphoric at what we had achieved. It turned out he was from Sharkeya, a rural governorate some 80 kilometers from Cairo. He was a commerce graduate but worked as a plumber because he could not get a job using his degree. For the past 20 days he hadn't made a penny; nobody was too concerned with blocked water pipes as the revolution brewed. He had spent his meagre savings (less than US$150) buying food and water for himself and his parents.

He told me that he had borrowed money from his brother to be able to come to Tahrir to join the demonstrators. He had slept in the street, eaten handouts, gone to the toilet at Tahrir residents' homes and screamed "Yaskot Hosni Mubarak!" (Down with Mubarak!) until his throat was sore. Two of his friends had come with him, both college graduates, one of them also a plumber. The other ran a small electric-appliances store with his father and brothers, selling toasters, kettles and the like. The three of them had taken an eight-hour journey to Cairo, on a minibus, on foot, on top of buses and in taxis, to come to Tahrir Square and join the revolution.

~

This was not a "revolution of the hungry". I met business people worth billions on the street. It was not a revolution by the Muslim Brotherhood; Christians were everywhere from day one. It was not just a "revolution by the youth"; young and old were here every day. This was not a revolution by the residents of Cairo; all over Egypt from Alexandria to Suez, Aswan and Sharkeya, everybody was involved. This was a revolution by all Egyptians for the freedom of all Egyptians from the regime of the last Pharaoh.

Cairo
March 25th, 2011

WHAT LED TO JANUARY 25ᵀᴴ?

Annemarie Evans

January 25ᵗʰ marked the first day of 18 that led to the fall of President Hosni Mubarak. That demonstration was the culmination of a number of protests that had been taking place for months, and even years. But the momentum that built from that day was the result of distinct socio-economic factors that brought hundreds of thousands of people on to the streets. For a long period prior to January and February's momentous events, opposition groups had demonstrated, there had been workers' strikes and protests that had been put down.

What makes the Egyptian revolution, which is still ongoing, so interesting is that the protesters who came on to the streets and gathered in Tahrir Square were all from different classes. This was a political revolution in which many social classes participated. Previous protests led by opposition groups such as Kefaya (which means "enough") had generated small turnouts, often severely outnumbered by Central Security Forces (CSF). But this time, the demonstrators far outnumbered the police.

Workers striking and turning out into the streets to protest had, for several years, been an important development in terms of political mobilization. But this was a multi-class revolution. The date, January 25ᵗʰ, was not a coincidence. It was chosen with intentional irony by opposition groups including Kefaya, who had organized the protest weeks in advance as it was national Police Day.

Depending on who you talk to, there are a host of reasons why

Egyptians wanted regime change. Mubarak had kept the country under a state of emergency since 1981 and had turned it into a police state. There was acute poverty, many graduates could not find jobs, and there was endemic corruption. While there had been economic growth, the government paid off its cronies in an atmosphere of narrow favoritism to keep Mubarak's failing government in power—an economic environment that choked out foreign investment.

Corruption is a huge problem that affects daily life, although subsequent to Mubarak's departure some senior businessman have been detained to face the courts. But it is prevalent throughout every layer of society. To get anything done, you needed to bribe officials, administrators and the police. If you had money and power, you were fine. For those with neither, daily life is a continual, grinding struggle. While there was economic growth during Mubarak's tenure, that did not translate to the street nor did it benefit most of the population.

While corruption has been rife for years, there were also specific triggers that moved the populace in more recent months. In mid-2010, a young man Khaled Said was arrested in a café in Alexandria by policemen, then beaten to death nearby. His head was crushed and a shocking image of his disfigured body went viral on the Internet. Though not an isolated incident, this particular case led to a series of protests and online campaigns, and public anger erupted over the fact that police could act with such impunity, with no fear of facing any justice.

The earlier revolt in Tunisia and the resignation of its president also ignited real fervor for change in Egypt. If it was possible to oust the president there, could it happen in Egypt?

When Mubarak came to power after the assassination of President Anwar Sadat in 1981, his government received revenues from oil, foreign aid and the Suez Canal. But during his rule these resources weakened and decreased. Citing the security of the country, Mubarak kept the nation permanently under a state of emergency, his point strengthened (he felt) by Islamist attacks in the 1990s. But while Egypt received military aid from the United States, other countries felt less inclined to invest.

While Egypt's relationship with Israel was viewed favorably by the US, it increasingly angered the Egyptian population. Egypt still looks with great pride to its army's actions during the 1973 Arab-Israeli War, which led to the return of the Sinai from Israel to Egypt. This was seen as a great psychological victory by Egyptians. But throughout Mubarak's tenure there were times when the people felt angered by Mubarak's obsequience to Israel and Egypt's cooperation on Israel's hardline treatment of the Palestinians.

World Bank statistics show that 40 per cent of the Egyptian population is below the poverty line, existing often on less than US$2 a day. Food and housing prices had become prohibitively high. Egypt's demographics would prove to be another factor. Up to 70 per cent of the population is under 30 years of age—hence the high proportion of youth ready to spill into the streets. There was high unemployment. Hundreds of young graduates competed for just a few jobs.

Samer Soliman, a professor of political economy at the American University of Cairo, explains that the public dissatisfaction that led to Mubarak being ousted also stemmed from increased taxation: Mubarak was taxing the people and paying off his cronies in an atmosphere of favoritism. Soliman posits that the revolution to oust Mubarak was far less of a surprise than the fact that Mubarak managed to hold on to power for so long while his government and country crumbled.

Mubarak increasingly taxed the population to solve the problems of a budget deficit, but the tax increased the conflict between the government and its citizens. "If you increasingly tax the people, the population is going to ask for more democracy and accountability. No taxation without representation," says Professor Soliman. "This was particularly relevant to the people participating in the revolution who watched the state of services deteriorate. The state gave fewer subsidies, services and healthcare to the poor. The capacity of the regime to spend money to increase its support decreased over the past 20 years. The state's carrot was shrinking under Mubarak."

But perhaps the biggest trigger for the revolution was police repression and brutality under Mubarak's emergency law. There was widespread use of torture, and Egypt had turned into a police state.

"Dignity was a key word used in the revolution," says Professor Soliman. "The last election in November was an important turning point. Three months prior to the revolution there had been parliamentary elections where the ruling party decided to clear parliament of the opposition." With the rigged elections so stacked in the ruling party's favor, people realized that there was no way to reform the government from within. "The revolution was the accumulation of a long process of mobilization and political attempts to remove the regime. It was a political revolution. It was not a class revolution. At the same time I cannot but acknowledge that it has socio-economic roots."

Egypt's revolution has some way to go in providing the democracy and voice that millions of demonstrators demanded. The president was the figurehead, but the people wanted to bring down the *regime*, not just Mubarak. Egypt will take some time to end military rule and make the transition to democracy. The revolution lacked a unified opposition, Professor Soliman observes, but the upshot is that there are now many more people and groups who have become politicized, representing different interests and demonstrating to demand their rights.

Now it is a matter of watching and safeguarding the evolution of those demonstrations from January and February 2011.

LIFE UNDER MUBARAK

Hatem Rushdy

Many people have asked me why I felt it necessary to participate in the revolution. As the owner of a successful and growing business, I should have had little to complain about. But the truth is that for me and many of the other revolutionaries, these 18 days and the results we hoped for had little to do with our bank accounts.

Life in Egypt under Mubarak was unbearable. Many higher-income Egyptians have spent time abroad for education, vacationing or business. They had seen how life could be and liked what they saw. Why shouldn't we choose our own governments and representatives? Why shouldn't our country be less corrupt, more transparent, less dirty and ugly, more free and fair? Why should our politicians not pay for their mistakes? Why should our police force not treat us respectfully? Why, among all the nations of the world, should we be robbed blind of our national wealth with no recourse?

Losing Dignity as a Country

Egyptians are a proud people. We have the richest and oldest civilization. During the reign of president Hosni Mubarak, our pride was gradually eroded. Under Mubarak we saw our national dignity weaken and we did not like it. Key among the reasons for this was the increasingly dependent role Egypt was playing in regional politics. Every year it seemed we were becoming less Arab and more American. Mubarak's co-operation in the Israeli occupation of Palestinian land and treatment of the Palestinian people were continuous sources of anger and disgrace among many Egyptians who, for historic and religious reasons, have always held Palestine close to their hearts. His closing of the Rafah border with Palestine—frequently the only path to Gaza for food, medicine and other basic goods—was met with many demonstrations here over the years. Egyptians resented that our foreign policy was dictated by either America or Israel.

When construction began last year on a wall between the Egyptian and Palestinian parts of the border city of Rafah, Egyptians again bemoaned the weak will of our president. The wall, it was rumored, was the brainchild of Israeli Prime Minister Benjamin Netanyahu and was designed and paid for by the Americans. The word on the street was that Israel was building a wall on one side of the Palestinians, and Egypt was closing them in by building a wall on the other side. Egyptians were angered by photographs of a smiling Mubarak shaking hands and sipping tea with Netanyahu as the latter ordered his army to pour phosphorous bombs on Palestinians throughout the offensive on Gaza last year, with American F-15s used to attack children armed with stones.

Over the years, at a rate of about once every six months, an Israeli soldier would randomly shoot dead an Egyptian border policeman and all Mubarak's government would do was ask the Israelis to carry out an investigation, the results of which were never publicized. No apology was demanded or received and certainly no reciprocal act was ever taken, not so much as the calling back of an ambassador. Egyptians were growing weary of this weakness and servitude.

Not only politically did there appear to be a lack of independence, but also economically. For years Egypt had been selling natural gas to Israel at a fraction of the international price. Opposition papers wrote articles on the billions of dollars lost annually because of the deal made with the Israelis which fixed prices for 30 years and was brokered by Mubarak's close friend Hussein Salem, now on Interpol's wanted list on behalf of the Egyptian government. The anger escalated in the summer of 2010 when Cairo had a series of power cuts due to low natural gas supplies. Mubarak ran the country not like its most senior civil servant, but like its owner.

But it was not only Egypt's ties with Israel that was causing this sense of collective indignity; even relations with Arab countries were flawed. The Egyptian government did nothing when, after a football game in Algeria, Egyptian fans were beaten and, at another football game in Sudan, attacked and several killed. When Egyptian workers in Gulf Arab countries complained to our embassies of mistreatment or not getting their salaries at the hands of their employers, again nothing happened.

Almost monthly, Egyptians drowned as they risked their lives trying to get across the Mediterranean to Europe's ports. Egyptians were dying trying to escape Mubarak's Egypt.

Despotic Security Forces

While the Egyptian government maintained a weak foreign policy, Mubarak's henchmen turned Egypt into a police state, consisting of a police force, State Security apparatus and Secret Service, all of which have brutally suppressed ordinary Egyptians. A man could be jailed for weeks for wanting to pray in a mosque, without being charged or standing trial. He could also face torture. This was the path that the internationally docile Mubarak government followed in dealing with its own citizens.

I personally know a young man who was arrested and jailed for six years. He was acquitted in court four times during that period and State Security would arrest him immediately upon his release (he never actually left prison; he was re-arrested before the release procedures were completed). His crime was that he lived in the same street as a suspected terrorist and that he prayed regularly at the local mosque. Under emergency law, (more on that below), State Security did not need to have an official, formal charge before arresting him; they could do it based on suspicion alone. Suspicion, in this case, was based on his address. This young man was routinely spat on, slapped and kicked, and occasionally beaten, electrocuted, sleep-deprived, forced to shower in freezing water in winter and made to urinate and defecate in the same three-meter-by-three-meter cell he shared with three others. For good measure, when one day he refused to sign a confession, State

Security brought in his mother (at the time over 60 years old) and let her talk to him. They threatened to put her in a cell overnight with 10 policemen. Needless to say, he signed the confession.

This I admit was extreme behaviour; the vast majority of Egyptians have not been raped or tortured by their own police force. But even in daily life, Egyptian police dealt with Egyptians with contempt. They often did not look you in the face, and used derogatory or insulting language when addressing you. They could also turn violent without provocation. A policeman could push, slap, hit or punch anybody with complete impunity. Any Egyptian could be treated this way. For example, many of the higher echelons of the Muslim Brotherhood are wealthy business people, but it never stopped the government from randomly arresting them and terrorising their families.

The police, through the various security bodies, were there to protect the regime from collapsing, not to protect the people from criminals. This was symbolized a few years back when the police changed its motto from "The Police: Serving the People", to "The Police and the People: Serving the Nation". Subsequent to the revolution, the original motto has been re-instated.

The Emergency Law allowed for this kind of behaviour and had been in place since president Anwar Sadat's assassination in 1981. How could you have a state of emergency for three decades? This legislation allowed State Security unbelievable powers to detain and question people without an arrest warrant; to forcefully enter and search (and frequently loot) people's homes with no authorization and to ignore court rulings to free political prisoners. Every few years, Mubarak would promise to amend or revoke the Emergency Law, but it never happened. Finally, a few years ago, he made a serious promise to modify it so it only covered terrorism and drug trading, but that too never happened.

So, for 30 years, we have lived under the threat of State Security, legalized by the Emergency Law with no recourse of any kind.

Skyrocketing Prices, Widening Income Gaps

The last decade or so has witnessed a simultaneous spike in

inflation, increase in unemployment and stagnation of all but a minority of people's incomes. This has put immense pressure on families. Food prices, housing costs, healthcare expenses and school fees have become prohibitive.

At the same time as rising prices were putting pressure on Egypt's middle class, the lower classes were suffering terribly. Photographs of children looking for food in rubbish dumps and stories of families who only have a meal every other day were filling the papers. One story about two years ago told of a Minister of Education official who was visiting a poor neighborhood school. The children were lined up in the playground for his visit when one girl fainted and fell to the ground. The teachers helped her to her feet and when she finally came to, the official talked to her and jokingly asked her what she had had for breakfast. The girl (six or seven years old) innocently replied that she hadn't had anything because it wasn't her turn. After further questions, the official understood that the girl had two siblings and that they took turns having breakfast, so that each of them would get the morning meal every third day. There were newspaper stories of fathers committing suicide because they couldn't pay the school fees or buy school uniforms or supplies, or get jobs or pay rent.

All this, while gated compounds pornographically advertised villas for *only* three or four or five million Egyptian pounds. "Now Within Your Reach", the advertisements read! One advertisement read, "So Everybody Can Afford It, the New Jaguar, Down to ONLY 666,000 Egyptian pounds". The combination of steep inflation, unemployment and increasing wealth for one or two per cent of the population was another of the pressures of Mubarak's Egypt. To be poor in a poor country is one thing; to be poor while the rich get richer at your expense is another.

When one day an opposition paper published the names of tens of Egypt's wealthiest businessmen and announced that they were not among the country's 1,000 highest tax-payers, people wondered, "Is it only the poor who are taxed?"

And it wasn't only the lowest-income groups that were feeling the squeeze. Professionals and small- and medium-sized business owners felt it too, seeing their efforts eroded through inflation. People who were not so unfortunate as to be unemployed saw their standard of living diminish in the face of insanely rising prices. What one could afford in January in some cases became unattainable by June.

What angered us was that we were expected to tighten the belt a few notches, not because Egypt was a poor country, or because the government was applying austerity measures, or because there was a solid plan to alleviate the suffering, but because the country was being robbed blind of its wealth through the corrupt practices of our government.

Severe Corruption

Saying that corruption was rampant in Mubarak's Egypt is tantamount to saying that water is wet. Corruption was a way of life before January 25th. From the five-pound note routinely crumpled into a traffic policeman's palm while shaking his hand to avoid a fine, to ministers demanding and receiving millions of pounds in bribes over the years for granting permits under their authority—that was how things operated. In 2009, Egypt ranked 111th out of 180 countries in Transparency International's Corruption Perceptions Index. A glaring example of corruption was the last parliamentary elections of 2010. Of the 400-plus seats won by Mubarak's National Democratic Party out of a total 454, a full 80 per cent were disputed in court over allegations of electoral fraud and bribery. Of those, more than 100 seats were nullified by court and yet the members of parliament continued to serve with complete disregard for the law, the courts and their rulings. When asked about this in a newspaper interview, Mubarak's cheeky response was along the lines that he never interfered in the workings of Egypt's judiciary.

Another area of corruption in the past decade has been the selling of construction land to government cronies for a fraction of the market price. With a young and fast-growing population, Egypt has a continuously growing need for housing and, as a result, construction is a very profitable business. The limiting factor has always been land. Over the past decades, the government sold thousands of acres of housing project land to construction firms for very low prices. The developers in turn would build the houses and then sell them at exorbitant prices. So high were housing prices in Egypt that a friend once calculated that for the same square footage, it is cheaper to buy a beach-front property in Florida than a flat in Cairo. Why did the government sell the land so cheaply? The simple answer is that the property developers would pay the low price officially, but then pay a bribe of 10-15 per cent of the real value to whoever was concluding the sale. One previous minister of development (the ministry responsible for the sale of government land) made so much money through these bribes that he, his wife, his two children, his brother-in-law and his nephews each owned multi-million pound houses in eight different gated communities.

A Failing Country

This corruption, inflation, despotism and loss of our collective dignity eventually led to a failing state. Egypt was slowly collapsing under Mubarak. The government under Mubarak was so focused on protecting its own existence, and so concentrated on the systematic plundering of the nation's wealth, that it had no time or interest in developing or even maintaining the country and its citizens.

Government health spending was so low that we have some of the highest kidney failure, diabetes and hepatitis rates on earth. Likewise, government spending on education was so low that while we have officially at least 26 per cent illiteracy, often graduates from government schools can barely read and write after completing their intermediary education, and graduates from state universities are among the least educated in the world. People have died in clashes in queues while waiting to buy bread. We had a severe bread crisis in Egypt a few years ago, which lasted more than three years. Some have died fighting in queues to buy butane gas bottles for cooking, and others from carcinogenic or expired food imported by corrupt traders with a blind eye turned by bribed government inspectors. Still others have died in collapsing apartment buildings, constructed using low-grade cement, again under the less-than-watchful eyes of government building inspectors.

Most recently, Cairo's streets—and those of other cities—have been plagued by yet another manifestation of corruption: garbage piles. After contracting several international garbage collection companies, the government stopped paying its dues and the garbage collection stopped.

So here we were, rich and poor alike, living in a country with garbage knee-high in some areas, with no say in who governs us, a country which was daily losing national pride, where despotism was rampant, inflation was out of control, where food could be scarce and reliable health services available only to the exceedingly wealthy, and where corruption was an accepted practice.

~

This was life under Mubarak. Was it all his fault? The Russians have a saying: A fish rots from the head, and then the rot works its way down. So yes, it was.

On the first day of our revolution, people carried banners calling for "Bread, Freedom and Dignity."

That says it all.

STORIES FROM
EGYPT'S REVOLUTION

Note: The conclusion of each of the following first-hand accounts is presented in the chapter titled "The Moment He Quit"

IT TOOK US ALL DAY TO BREAK
THROUGH THE BARRICADES

Mansour Abdel Ghaffar

Mansour Abdel Ghaffar is a lawyer with a PhD in jurisprudence. He is in his mid-forties and lives in Cairo with is wife and children. Protesting alongside his colleagues from the Lawyers' Syndicate, Mr. Abdel Ghaffar found himself daily in the thick of fighting and tear-gas attacks. He witnessed security officers setting fire to their own vehicles in order to implicate the demonstrators. He also witnessed the bravery of youth and women. On February the 2nd, he counted 22 dead.

~

It was clear from the beginning that this was not a normal demonstration. In previous protests, there would be 100 people at most and the security forces would surround us in overwhelming numbers and maybe arrest one or two protesters. That day, Tuesday, January 25th, when we all met in front of the Supreme Court, there must have been at least 2,000 of us. It took us all day to break through the barricades that the security forces had made around us. We walked towards Tahrir Square but when we got to the corner of Ramses Street, they started attacking us with tear gas to disperse us. They were successful; we started breaking up into small groups and running from them into the side streets. We could tell they were getting exhausted, because they would go into side streets and sit down to rest, which made sense as they were carrying heavy shields and clubs, and wearing helmets.

By nighttime I was getting tired myself. But I wanted to carry on demonstrating and so I did not go home; I made it to the Lawyers' Syndicate building nearby. I was exhausted and I slept in the building, together with about a hundred or so fellow lawyers. I thought it would be safer than being on the street. This was a big mistake. The next morning, the police, knowing that many people were hiding inside the building, fired four tear-gas bombs inside. Everybody started to choke and we were barely able to get into the small garden outside, but the open air was very heavy with tear gas and we were still choking. What made things worse was that they were not allowing us off the premises. We were trapped and the tear gas was getting really bad. Then a large number of people managed to break through the rows of policemen who were blocking the entrance to the Syndicate. They freed us and we were able to get out onto the street.

When we left the building we found hundreds of young demonstrators, both men and women, sitting in the street and blocking it. They were refusing to let traffic move. My lawyer colleagues and I tried to convince them to get off the street and go on the sidewalks to allow traffic to move. We walked over to them and a police officer stopped us, warning us not to join them in the middle of the street. We told him we just wanted to persuade them to move. So he let us get through to them and we were arguing with the young men and women that they should get off the street and that this was an uncivilized way to demonstrate, but they refused to move. They said if they got up the police would separate them and beat them up individually and that it was safer to stay there together.

Then, suddenly, as we were talking, the police attacked us with their clubs. The lawyers were the first to get hit and we were beaten viciously, on the head, on the back; people got hit in different places. At this point, the police grabbed five lawyers, all colleagues of mine, and threw them into a minibus. We chased them before the minibus took off and managed to get them out after a scuffle. We then started walking towards Tahrir Square again, but the security police were very aggressive and the tear gas was so heavy, I ran back to the Syndicate to hide once more. We spent the night going in and out of the building because we were afraid they would tear-gas us again, so we alternated between the Syndicate and the street.

On Thursday the 27th, everybody was saying we must get to Tahrir to be there for Friday's call for a Day of Rage. Some people got through but many were arrested and three were killed, one of whom I knew. He was called Youssry and was a law graduate. He had been very intent on getting to Tahrir. We tried to convince him after all the beatings and the tear gas that it might be better to wait for Friday prayers the next day and then for all of us to go to Tahrir, but he was insistent. He left us and we received news of his killing late on Thursday, close to midnight. May God have mercy on his soul. I am sure he died a martyr. That night, Thursday night, I spent the night in my office in Dokki [on the western bank of the Nile, opposite downtown Cairo]. I called home to tell my wife that I had too much work and couldn't come home that night. I did not tell her that I was participating in the demonstrations. I did not want to worry her.

The next morning, Friday the 28th, I decided to go to al-Fath Mosque in Ramses for my prayers. I heard later that there was a long list of mosques and churches that were to be meeting points for demonstrators, but I had not received this message for some reason. I knew that this was a mosque close to Tahrir and also that it had been the starting point of many prior demonstrations. The mosque was full, so I bought a newspaper and spread its pages on the street and sat on it with several people. The sermon was very balanced; the imam said the demonstrators were just asking for their rights. He also urged all demonstrators to behave in a peaceful and civilized manner and not to destroy any property or get violent with the police. He also addressed the police themselves, asking them to deal in a humane manner with the demonstrators, saying, "They are your brothers and sisters; we are all Egyptian," and things like that. Right after prayers, I saw a lawyer who was also an ex-member of parliament. He was praying with us outside the mosque and as soon as we finished, he quoted the Quran aloud: "Pharaoh and Haman and their soldiers were wrongful!" [This is a reference to Mubarak and his head of police.]

Then he shouted, "Allah Akbar!"

Then the protest chants started: "Yaskot, Yaskot Hosni Mubarak!" (Down, Down with Hosni Mubarak!), "Yaskot, Yaskot el-Toghyan!" (Down, Down with Tyranny!) and, of course, "Al-Shaab Yureed Eskat el-Nezam!" (The People Want to Topple the Regime!). There must have been at least 3,000 people in the mosque, all there to demonstrate. I think everyone was planning to go to Tahrir Square. There were hundreds of riot police right outside of the mosque gates and so people started jumping over the fence surrounding the mosque. The police were hitting those who jumped over the fence with their sticks. I got hit on the back while I was jumping over.

We lined up facing the Central Security police. The police commander shouted that he would not allow us to block traffic or cause chaos on the street. A few of us shouted back that we were not planning to block traffic, that we would be happy to walk on the sidewalk so long as they left us alone and let us get to Tahrir Square in peace. He yelled back sarcastically that he and his men were not there to escort us to Tahrir. Then one of the demonstrators shouted: "Why do you people continue to refuse reason? We are not asking for an escort, just for you to let us through. When will you start being sensible?" This seemed to enrage the police commander and he yelled, "Fire!" They started firing tear gas at us and we were defenseless.

We tried to push them back a little just to allow us some space to run but it was almost impossible; they attacked us viciously to keep us in the tight space in front of the mosque. We finally managed to push them back just until the next traffic lights and then we ran off into the side streets leading to the district of Sabteya. As we walked through Sabteya, people kept joining our demonstration. And people started throwing onions to us from their balconies and handing us bottles of vinegar, so we would be able to sniff them to help against the pain of the tear gas. We truly felt that the people who could not join us wanted to help in some way.

We ended up getting onto the Nile Corniche, alongside the Ministry of Foreign Affairs, and there we found a huge blockade set up by Central Security policemen. They attacked us with tear gas and water cannons and we could not get through, so we got split up again. I ended up walking with five or six other guys on the side streets behind the Ministry. People called out to us from balconies, telling us where to go to avoid the police. They would tell us which streets were blocked. We ended up back on the Nile Corniche and found many other demonstrators there, too. We walked together along the Nile towards Tahrir Square again. Many of the younger protesters were beginning to get angry. We had been chased, beaten, tear-gassed, some people had been arrested. Some of the younger guys were losing it. They wanted revenge; they wanted to break up tiles off the sidewalk or take stones off the streets and smash things. But the older people were being sensible. They told them that any property they damage is ours, not the government's, and all of it would have to be rebuilt using our tax money. The youngsters seemed to be convinced and calmed down.

As we approached the state-television building, we were confronted again by blockades of Central Security policemen and officers. We decided to try a different approach. We thought of sending three older, sensible men to talk to the police officers, to explain that we were not looking for trouble and that we just wanted to get to Tahrir. We thought maybe they would listen to reason.

While the three men were talking to the commander of the force, some policemen grabbed one of the men and took him behind their lines and we could see them beating him up. This drove the demonstrators nuts. How could they beat up an older man who was just there to negotiate with them? We could no longer maintain control or ask the demonstrators to stay calm and peaceful, and they started taking stones off the street and throwing them almost randomly. I have to be honest, cars were damaged and maybe other property; people were really just going wild with anger and throwing stones everywhere. This angry attack helped us get through that barricade and we ended up in Ramses Square. Things were much quieter there. The demonstrators were completely in control of the square and we could not see a single policeman. It was very strange.

So we walked on towards Tahrir, and every few hundred

meters we found a burned Central Security transport truck. We found maybe ten of them set on fire and left to burn on the street. Then as we walked on, we came upon a number of Central Security officers who were burning another truck. It was very clear to everyone: they were setting their own vehicles on fire. I am willing to testify to this in court. I pointed at them and yelled, "I can see you and you can see me, and I now know your face. You are setting your own cars on fire to blame the demonstrators." When we got to Abdel Moneim Riad Square, we could not get in to Tahrir Square from there directly; we had to go through side streets, but finally we managed to get into the square. Soon after we got in, they seemed to block even the side streets; now we were inside and surrounded from every direction. It felt like we were in a very large trap. Tahrir that day was like a battlefield. You could see blood in many places, people being carried away from the front line. It was unbelievable, like you would see on television in Iraq or Palestine.

There were three groups of demonstrators. One was at Abdel Moneim Riad Square, another in the middle of Tahrir Square and a third near the American University. I went straight to the group at Abdel Moneim Riad Square and I saw death there. Police officers were shooting at people; they were trying to run them over with their vehicles, big blue ones with water cannons on top. And the demonstrators, these brave men, had nothing but their bodies with which to face this assault. It even sounded like a war. Bullets, screams, stones being thrown and falling on cars. People shouting "Allah Akbar!" It was surreal, unbelievable. We reached the Egyptian Museum and there was a burned-down police truck. We put out the fire and pushed the truck so it was parked sideways across the street. This was the very first form of barricade we could find to hide behind to avoid being shot at, and to throw stones back at the police. We thought this must be how the Palestinians feel when all they have are stones and the opposition is firing at them with real weapons.

We all fought hard not to let the police through Abdel Moneim Riad Square, because we knew they would massacre the people in Tahrir. Many people died that day, many who knew they would die. Going towards Abdel Moneim Riad Square was like suicide, but backing down would mean many would be killed in Tahrir. We could not let them advance towards the square. Things slowly settled and there was no longer any trouble, or at least it did not seem imminent that the police were going to break through into Tahrir Square from the Abdel Moneim Riad side.

I then went towards the American University area and Qasr el-Einy Street with another group. We had heard that there was a huge police force coming from that direction and the demonstrators blocking that area needed support, so we ran over there. We found another truck; someone unlocked the brakes and we were able to push it towards the middle of the road to act as a barrier. I hid behind that truck and there was a young man sitting next to me. In the middle of bouts of shooting, he was trying to joke with me to relieve the tension. He asked me: "Does Hosni Mubarak have two wives? Because if he does, it must be really difficult. Revolution on the streets and two women at home to handle!" I couldn't believe it. There was live ammunition fire, we had seen many killed in the past hours, yet he was smiling and trying to make light of the situation.

A little after midnight, we had started—this young man and I—to swap shifts. He would collect stones and hand them to me to throw for a while and when my shoulder started to hurt, we would switch. During one of my throwing shifts, I reached behind me for stones, but nothing was laid into my hand. I looked back and found this lovely, funny man dead on the ground with a bullet in his head. I went hysterical. I got up from my hiding spot and I couldn't help myself. In hindsight, I realize I could have been shot too, but at the time I was going crazy, I did not know what to do. I was screaming, "This kid is dead, this kid is dead— he's been shot in the head!" Of course nobody could come to help us or do anything, because our hiding spot was already under fire.

I got out from behind the car, carrying stones in both hands, and started running towards the police. I hurled the stones as hard as I could, and was running and throwing almost blindly. It was crazy. Many people came towards me to help me and I am sure this is what saved me. They were all throwing stones at the policemen and we chased them up the street towards the Parliament building. One of the policemen turned around and fired a round from his shotgun at us. I ducked as quickly as I could but caught a pellet in the forehead, which really hurt, but I think because of the distance it did not penetrate my skull. I also felt pellets grazing the top of my head, so I guess I had leaned down just in time. Blood was running down my face, but I no longer felt any pain. They took me to the field hospital to check if any of the pellet remained in my head, but it had merely broken my skin and made me bleed; physically, I was fine.

I went back to the same area of Qasr el-Einy and we battled these people all night. We threw stones and whatever else we could find as they shot at us. But, thank God, by the end of that night, before dawn on Saturday the 29th, we had taken over and secured the whole of Tahrir Square. We had completely removed the Central Security policemen from the square. We captured 20 or more of them and surrounded them and they thought we were going to kill them. To their surprise we gave them food, even though we hardly had any food at all. A few of them were injured, so we took them to the field hospital already set up in the square. Most of them said they did not want to go back to the police and asked us for clothes so they could leave without being identified by the demonstrators or by their superiors. We gave them whatever clothes we could find; someone had a jacket, someone else gave a T-shirt he was wearing under his shirt or his pullover and we let them go. They left everything—their helmets, their army boots, their shields, batons and sticks, everything— and they left the square. We did nothing to them. Some of them cried because of the good treatment they received.

The next morning, starting at maybe 8am, a few young men were very excited and went a bit crazy. They wanted to move to the Ministry of Interior and take it over. The older ones among us tried to talk sense into them. We tried to explain that leaving the square would make it more vulnerable, because there would be fewer people to defend it. But they didn't listen. They insisted that the Ministry of Interior had to be taken over. In the end there was nothing we could do to stop them, and a large number—I don't know, maybe a few hundred—insisted on going. They went in batches to try to storm the ministry and returned with their dead and wounded. Many died in the attempt to take over the ministry. That day, we found out there were snipers on top of the ministry. I understood that this was the policemen's last stand; we had kicked them out of Tahrir Square, out of Ramses Square, out of the surrounding areas, so they had no place to go except the ministry. We told the young men all of this, but they would not listen. Ten or fifteen guys would go, but six or seven would come back, the rest shot dead. They tried this many times but failed every time.

All through that Saturday, police and thugs tried over and over to get into Tahrir Square, but we resisted and were successful in keeping the square secure. People inside knew or felt that if the square fell, the police would kill everyone inside. For the next three days—right through Monday the 31st—there was a stand-off. We held the square and nobody was trying to get in any longer. On those three days, we had almost no food. Some people tried to sneak food in to us.

On Tuesday, February the 1st, we heard that Mubarak was to make a speech later in the day. Of course we all had very high hopes for that speech. We really believed he would listen to the people and resign. But, of course, as we all know now, the whole speech was an act of deception, trying to take advantage of how kind-hearted we Egyptians are. He said things like: "I am an old man; I was never planning to run for the presidency in September anyway; I want to die here; I have done a lot for this country..." And being kind-hearted, many Egyptians believed him. I am sorry to say this about my people, but we are soft-hearted and kind to the point of being foolish sometimes. You know what? Napoleon Bonaparte himself, who invaded Egypt and stole from us and killed Egyptian people, made a sentimental speech when he was finally being driven out of Egypt. We are such a soft-hearted race that some Egyptians cried during *that* speech. This is how kind and gentle-hearted we are. Napoleon! He occupied us and killed Egyptians, yet we cried at his sentimental speech.

Anyway, after Mubarak's speech, we became very depressed. Like I said, many people, maybe even most people, had thought that he was going to resign so, of course, the expectations were very high. We all hoped that he would just listen to the people and leave. But then during the speech it became clear that he was not going to resign; he said he wanted to stay on as president until September and then not run again for elections. People were bitterly disappointed. For me, I had a bigger problem than disappointment. I saw people within the square who were being swayed by his speech. Some people even began arguing with me, "What more do we want? He will not run again; he will appoint a vice-president. The man has done a lot for the country; he fought wars for the country." They were saying things like that. Also things like: "What is the problem with letting him leave with dignity? He is an old man; he just wants to leave in an honorable fashion. He does not want the humiliation of Zine al-Abidine Ben Ali (the Tunisian president who was ousted from his office and forced to flee the country). Why should we insist on insulting the symbol of our country?" Why this, why that? I was very unhappy with this talk.

Many people—myself among them—felt we were being fooled and that he was playing the sentimental card and that if we accepted and left Tahrir, then for sure, he would just go back on all his promises. He would say, "You see? The people want me to stay, they have left Tahrir." What happened after that speech was a splitting of the ranks in Tahrir: those who felt sorry for him and thought, why not let him stay till September, and (I think) the majority who still insisted that he must leave immediately. Some people left the square that night, thinking they had won their battle, but I didn't go anywhere. I knew this was just a ruse to fool us into believing him.

On Wednesday, February the 2nd, after he had made all these promises—"I will take care of this, protect that, assure the other thing"—we found ourselves under the most vicious attack since Friday. They came at us from all directions: from Qasr el-Nil, from the direction of the Egyptian Museum, from the direction of the American University. They seemed initially like regular demonstrators, who were there to support Mubarak. Some of them carried banners saying "Yes to Mubarak" and some chanted slogans which answered ours. For example we had a slogan saying "We Will Not Leave [Tahrir], He Will Leave [the presidency]!" and their counter was "He Will Not Leave, You Will Leave!"

Initially, it seemed as if they were just pro-Mubarak

demonstrators who were enthused by his speech the night before. Some of us went over to talk to them, explaining that the speech had not really changed anything. And at first, we had a civilized dialogue, each group expressing their opinions. Some of them actually began to listen to us and accept our point of view. But then from within the pro-Mubarak crowd, people came out who started urging them not to talk to us. I was sure they were State Security or from the National Democratic Party or something.

Then at around 2pm, a dozen men on horses and camels raced into the square. They were followed by hundreds of thugs wielding sticks and metal bars and broken-up ceramic tiles, and they started attacking us. It was clear to me that these were neither demonstrators nor pro-Mubarak activists. They were thugs. This was how the Battle of the Camel started.

When the camels and horses first came into the square, many young men threw themselves physically at the animals to get them to stop. Some got trampled and others got hit with swords that the riders were carrying. But in the end it was these men who managed to stop the camels and horses. That day, we captured six horses and a camel. A video posted on YouTube from that day shows Sheikh Safwat Hegazy [a well-known television cleric who was present in Tahrir throughout the revolution] riding one of the captured horses. I have to be honest, when we got the riders off their horses and camels, we beat them up viciously. One of them was hurt badly in his eye and he was saying, "All I got was 200 pounds, getting treatment for my eye will cost more than that." So it was clear that these were paid thugs, not sincere pro-Mubarak demonstrators.

This battle was to last until sunrise the next day. We had split ourselves into groups and each group started resisting. The crowd that had arrived first, the people whom I said seemed like genuine pro-Mubarak protesters, left as soon as the fighting started. We managed to evict the stragglers among them, who were on the sidelines. The only pro-Mubarak protesters now were those who had arrived when the horses and camels came in—they were the thugs. The biggest groups were coming from the direction of the Egyptian Museum and Abdel Moneim Riad Square. This is a very wide street, too wide to close off properly. There was a big

Riot police prepare for anticipated protests

construction site just before the museum. We went in and carried off all the wood and metal sheets and whatever else we could find to block the street with. We started forming blockades across this area. This also acted as a protective wall from behind which we could throw stones. We would throw stones for a while and when the thugs moved back we would push the barricades forward. We ended up with three barricades, one behind the other with maybe 50 meters between each one. This lasted for several hours.

By around 10pm, we had pushed them all the way out to the museum. This was not an easy process. People were killed. We saw big trucks from Abou Enein's factories come onto the bridge overlooking the square and they had hundreds of cartons of broken ceramic tiles. [Mohamed Abou el-Enein was a senior member of the National Democratic Party and one of the biggest manufacturers of ceramic tiles in Egypt and the Middle East.] The thugs were throwing these at us. These ceramic pieces were like shards. They had sharp edges and if you got hit with one, you would get seriously cut. I saw many people who got hurt this way.

Late in the evening, we had pushed the thugs all the way back to Abdel Moneim Riad Street. I was one of the first to get there. I was hiding behind a burned car and throwing stones from behind it. Right beside me, a young lady—a girl really, short and very thin—was energetically motivating us. She was throwing stones and was unstoppable. I tried with several others to dissuade her several times, telling her to fall back from the front. But there was no convincing her. In the end someone pushed her, almost hitting her for her own good, and they forced her to the back lines so she would not get herself killed.

We pushed the burned armored vehicle towards the Sixth of October Bridge and found a safe spot below, where they could not reach us anymore. We threw as many things as we could onto the bridge from below. Then a group of people—some were from the Muslim Brotherhood—decided to try and go on top of the bridge to remove the danger there. These men must have known that they would almost certainly die, because there was a large number of thugs on the bridge. When these men got on top of the bridge and started fighting, we felt it was safer to move out from beneath the bridge, but it turned out this was a mistake.

As we left the safety beneath the bridge, snipers started shooting people down. People were being hit in the head, in the heart, in the chest. They were not shooting people in the legs or arms, they were shooting to kill. It was a massacre. Many people fell that day. One man was shot in the stomach and as we carried him back to the field hospital, he said, "Put me down here, just protect the square, don't let these thugs get in." It was heroic.

I saw one incident that will remain with me until I die. One young man was trying to get on top of the bridge to join the others there and a sniper aimed his laser pointer at his chest. The young man saw the red dot, looked towards the sniper and opened his jacket as if to say, "Shoot me, I'm not afraid to die." The sniper shot him anyway. It was one of the saddest, bravest things I had ever seen.

It became clear to the snipers and other thugs on top of the bridge that they were fighting a losing battle, against people who did not care anymore what happened to them, who were willing to die. Things started calming down and by dawn there were no more people on top of the bridge, no snipers, nothing. We were up for the rest of the night, of course, still worried and scared that maybe more people were still going to come and attack us.

The next morning, it was like a scene from a war movie. Dead bodies, injured people, the field hospital overflowing, ambulances trying to leave Tahrir to get to nearby hospitals. Some ambulances were sent back by the police who were at the peripheries of Tahrir Square and were refused passage to the hospitals. They returned to the square and asked where to go or what to do because State Security was preventing them from getting to hospitals. What kind of sick people prevent ambulances from getting to hospitals? They must be punished for this, otherwise nobody who was in Tahrir can ever forgive them or treat any police officer like a human being again. We cannot forget the sights we saw. I can understand—not excuse, but understand—using tear gas to disband a demonstration, but preventing ambulances full of injured people from getting to hospital is beyond my comprehension.

I personally counted at least 22 dead that night and I would guess more than 1,000 were injured, some very seriously. That night we joked that if you got only ten stitches you were not really injured. My back was injured that day, but it was considered minor because I did not require stitches. It was worse than the first Friday of Rage, because it was an act of treachery—just the night before the president had promised all kinds of changes. The president and prime minister later denied that they had anything to do with the Day of the Camel.

The next day was very quiet. It was, in fact, so quiet and peaceful that I called my wife and told her to join me in the square. She came and saw the tents and our sleeping conditions and how I had been living for the past two weeks. Of course, I was very happy when people told her how brave I had been during all the battles we had; I am happy she can be proud of her husband.

Only when she came and asked me, "How were you eating? How were you sleeping?", did I actually think about it. We had been eating whatever food was available. If someone had something to eat, anyone could join in; they didn't even need to ask. If someone had a loaf of bread, he would take a tiny bite and pass it on, and so on until everyone had had a bite of it. A cup of tea would be passed around between maybe seven or eight people before it was finished. I think if we had tried this just two weeks before in Cairo, the first person would have gulped down the entire cup of tea without thinking about anyone else.

Behavior was changing; people were becoming selfless. I saw a man from Sharkeya with his friends; they were eating falafel and a loaf of bread. I had a bite of falafel and it satisfied me until the next day. On one of the first days we found a guy who had broken into McDonald's and stolen food. We sent him back with the food even though we had very little to eat. We insisted on staying clean and decent. People who managed to find a patch of grass on which to sleep were considered privileged, because most people were sleeping on the asphalt or cement sidewalks.

That night, on Thursday, February the 10th, the president made his speech. When he said he would not leave and that he would only delegate his powers to his vice-president, I actually passed out. I was unconscious for a few minutes I think. It was a complete shock to me after all that we had been through.

WE ARE CREATING
THE DRUMS OF WAR

Azza Tawfik

Azza Tawfik, a 42-year-old businesswoman and community volunteer, had dreamt of an Egypt where people showed respect for one another, where there was hope of a new and bright future that went beyond corruption and the fear embedded in a police state. While Egypt still faces upheaval and people have returned to Tahrir in recent months, for Ms. Tawfik walking round Tahrir Square during some of those 18 days gave her hope for her country that she had never trusted would happen in her lifetime, or at least not before Mubarak was dead. She met fellow countrymen who had often travelled hundreds of kilometers to be there and it made Ms. Tawfik believe in her country again. But the revolution came at a great cost. There have been more than 300 confirmed deaths and many more who disappeared. Two of Ms. Tawfik's friends disappeared from Tahrir Square; for 44 days their families could not find them. Their bodies were finally found at a hospital; they had been shot by snipers.

~

F riday, December 31ˢᵗ, 2010. New Year's Eve always brings thoughts of what we want the following year to bring. I wish for 2011 to be a year of purification, but my thoughts at this time do not exceed personal detoxification, general cleansing and better order in my life. The idea of leaving Egypt for a while to a more comfortable country was not far away from my thoughts, not because of selfishness but because of the daily trials of combating corruption everywhere. This has become the norm for me to such an extent that I am regarded as crazy by most people, because I cannot accept corruption. I refuse to pay bribes, and for that my life is often made very complicated even when I want the simplest thing done. Many people tell me I am asking for the impossible, that I must live with it and accept it.

New Year's Day, 2011. There is a deadly explosion at a church in Alexandria. Innocent people are killed while praying and celebrating the New Year. All I can think is, what a sad start to the year! Alexandria has been tense ever since a young man, Khaled Said, was killed by police officers here last year.

Friday, January 14th. Tunisian president Zine al-Abidine Ben Ali departs for Saudi Arabia following demonstrations all over the country. The news comes to me like a beautiful dream: a better tomorrow may be possible! I have gathered with others for a meditation weekend. Our instructor points out that we are supposed to be meditating, but there are too many questions on our minds. Most of us are happy with the news. We discuss it over dinner, asking many questions—in particular, is it possible for this to ever happen in Egypt? Even if Mubarak dies, I fully expect his son, Gamal, to take over and continue the corruption and suppression forever. I have often wondered where are the brave Egyptians these days who won back the Sinai following the Arab-Israeli war of 1973? Can they be among the Egyptian youth of today, who seem to only care about fun and drugs? The evening is full of discussion, and it is the first time I sense how heavily politics and the current sad situation in Egypt are on all our minds, even if we rarely spoke about it. I say that I hope Egypt is able to stand up to corruption, but I do not expect my wishes to come true as quickly as they do.

Friday, January 28th. What a day that I will live to remember!

I was unable to join the demonstrations before today because a sinusitis operation on the 19th left me weak for a few days. On January 25th, I watched the large crowds of demonstrators from my window and wished I was among them. I prayed I would be fit enough to join people in the streets by Friday.

Today, both the Internet and mobile networks were cut, but the ball has been rolling since the 25th and so we all know where to meet and what to do. It is a different feeling: getting dressed in sportswear, taking only my ID and enough money to get me back to Maadi, where I live. Looking out, I count huge numbers of Central Security cars in front of Galaa Bridge in Dokki, tens of secret security men all over the street, posted two meters apart, watching and sometimes stopping people. I kiss my dog goodbye, pray to be back safely and go to meet friends so that we can move in large groups. I can see eleven trucks belonging to the Central Security Forces (CSF)—large empty ones to load protesters into! I could be one of them. Mustn't think like that. Millions of questions in my mind. How are we going to cross all the barriers and go past all those officers to reach Tahrir Square?

Suddenly my eyes start to burn. Already, tear-gas bombs are being thrown around Cairo University to bar demonstrators coming out of Giza Mosque, where opposition politician Mohamed ElBaradei was praying. In a group of ten, my friends and I go back to the street and wait for demonstrations coming from Mohandiseen. Wow! They are coming over in huge numbers. Hope and power fill the air. We talk to people in the streets, ask them to join us, to be honest with themselves and stand up for their rights. Cheering against Mubarak feels great. The collective consciousness of the crowd is fabulous, immense!

The minute we reach Galaa Square, facing troops who are waiting for us, we have to stop as tear-gas bombs rain down upon us. A terrible experience and it hurts! I cannot believe I just had a sinus operation and here I am facing this much tear gas. I can't see where my friends are, I can't open my eyes. A stranger takes my hand and walks me to the side. How kind! Love and cooperation is growing among us all. Everybody is sharing their Coca-Cola or Pepsi, their bottles of water, and their vinegar and onion pieces. Oh how they saved me! I don't understand why I did not carry that stuff with me. Our spontaneous reply to the bombs is to cheer "Peaceful!", which seems to mean nothing to the police who are very generous with the tear gas. A few young men pick up canisters and throw them back at the police.

A short while afterward, the stock of tear gas is finished and we are able to get up on top of Qasr el-Nil Bridge. What a feeling! Protesters are standing on CSF trucks and calling out for us to cross the bridge. A couple of fast-thinking men are deflating the tyres and taking out the batteries. Good thinking! It's odd, though. With a new battle flaring up on the far side of the bridge, the police are letting us through. Sadly, it is not because they support us. They have run out of tear gas, so they are passing us along on the bridge and straight into a real battle. This is where I get hit in the arm by one of the canisters. We move away from the front lines; one of my friends is suffocating from all the tear gas and the crowds, so we wait on the side. There are many people getting injured at the front. There is blood all over the ground. People are running, carrying the injured, trying to rescue them and take them to any nearby hospital. Live bullets! They are now using live bullets, water cannons and incessant tear gas bombs. We all run in different directions, and of course I cannot see any of my friends. Later, I find two of them and we spend hours searching for the rest of the group.

A long battle ends with some dead, many injured and a totally exhausted crowd, but again the police retreat. With large groups of protesters joining us from the outskirts of Giza, we manage to cross into Tahrir Square. It feels so special, as though we are crossing the Suez Canal in 1973.

Sunday, January 30th. It is 8am and I'm walking around Tahrir Square, smiling happily while watching people around me: different groups of young and elderly people, women, men, artists, writers, politicians, activists, laborers, your average employees, poor people. The environment is so much like a fantastic festival. We are all Egyptians. We are all here for common causes: freedom, democracy and dignity.

There is a group of young people, all from different backgrounds. They are seated in a circle, singing old songs of the very special Sheikh Imam, enjoying slang poetry by the great poet Ahmed Fouad Negm. The group is getting bigger and attracting people from all walks of life. Maybe some of them have never heard of Sheikh Imam before today, but now they are feeling and appreciating his songs.

I pass by another group enjoying a religious discussion, sharing details and spiritual stories. Another group is discussing political issues, talking about the corruption each one has faced, each case enough to bring down this regime. Another group of young people is sitting and chatting next to a banner that calls for Mubarak to be put on trial. A group of artists is performing a satire about the current situation in Egypt. They have gathered an audience. Other groups roam the square chanting for the fall of the tyrant. All around me are different ideologies with one common dream—a beautiful mixture of people, forming a respectful community, one that I always dreamt of and never thought I would live to see.

The whole world sees that the Arab world is reborn and everybody around the world is proud of the Egyptians. I am proud of the Egyptians, too. I have found in Tahrir Square all that I was looking for, all that I have wished for Egypt to become. It is truly 'Independence Square'—or more specifically, it is Martyrs' Square.

I smile at my thoughts and look around at the young people in the square, the ones I doubted. They have an awareness that I did not expect, and such a civilized attitude. The protesters are becoming stronger and the government is becoming more stupid and blind, with more mistakes which will be their downfall. The end of the regime is what we dare to dream of, call for and insist on.

I touch my arm and it hurts. I had forgotten about the tear gas canister that hit me two days before. Thank God it did not hit me on the face—it really hurts.

During those early days I had time for reflection, but there is no time for that in the days to follow. Each day has its own special feature, but the common theme is danger, death and searching for lost friends. Ziad Bakir is a 37-year-old graphic designer and photographer working at the Cairo Opera House. He is the father of three children. Tarek Abdel Latif is an engineer in his mid-30s and the father of two. He works for a multinational oil company and is planning to emigrate soon with his family to Canada. Ziad and Tarek are lost; no one knows where they are for weeks. After their disappearance, members of their families come to the square nearly every day, hoping to hear news about them. Their bodies finally turn up in a hospital, more than 40 days later. They have been shot dead by snipers.

Wednesday, February 2nd. I am so angry today: it is an ugly day followed by an ugly night. It begins with armed thugs on camels and horses, and ends with continuous gunshots and hundreds of people seriously injured and many dead. At midday, we suddenly find ourselves under attack by crowds of pro-Mubarak thugs who come from the direction of the museum. That whole day we endure snipers on buildings, handmade bombs thrown at us from above, armed thugs trying to invade the square and get us all killed! I have been giving a daily eyewitness account to the BBC of the things I see, and this is the one day that leaves me totally enraged. Even if they kill us all, I will not leave until Mubarak is out of office.

Most of my friends have left. I spend the night helping fighters at the perimeters of the square by bringing them rocks and stones from within the square and by banging stones loudly on metal fences. We are creating the drums of war! In fact, this has a positive impact on all of us. With our small stones we manage to beat them— because we believe in our cause whereas these paid thugs do not. Who would want to die for 200 Egyptian pounds?

Two of my friends are still with me. One fights at the Champollion Street side and the other is a girl who stays with me near Qasr el-Nil Bridge. My friend gets hit in the eye and we have to see a doctor at the hospital, which is a mosque transformed into a field clinic, with volunteer doctors and donated medical tools.

Thursday, February 3rd. We are exhausted this morning. We have had no sleep and very little food. We are so happy, though, to see the people arriving in Tahrir since early morning, bringing in food, medical supplies, blankets and water. One of them is a boy, no older than 14 years old, who has come on his own from the Pyramids area carrying two huge bags of baked goods. It is a dangerous thing for him to do. He left his home at 6am, arriving in Tahrir four hours later.

God, I love these people. We deserve a better country and these young people deserve a better future. The level of love and solidarity I see and feel this morning is enough to help me recharge and continue. I borrow clothes from a friend of mine who lives in Dokki because it is impossible for me to go back to Maadi where I live; I would not be able to come back or I might get arrested. I know absolutely that my mobile is being monitored by State Security.

Despite all the deaths and injuries, there is still a great mood inside Tahrir Square. I have met some very interesting characters whom I will never forget:

Rabeea: This man is badly hurt in one eye and one leg, but this does not stop him from cleaning the streets in Tahrir. He was injured during his repeated attempts to collect the bodies of those who were shot in Lazoghly, near the Ministry of Interior and State Security headquarters.

Ahmed from Marsa Matrouh: He traveled 600 kilometers from northern Egypt to join us in Tahrir. A young student in his second year of college, he dreams of a better future for his country, and like many in Egypt, of a life without corruption and a thieving government. He participated in the demonstrations in Alexandria, but then came to join us like many others in Tahrir.

Om Ahmed: An elderly mother of five, she has decided that the only thing that she can do for her children's future is join us in Tahrir. It is very interesting how clearly an old, illiterate woman can think! She left them at home and did not tell any of her neighbors what she was up to and she came. The army soldiers did not let her in. Funny, they told her, "Why would a kind woman like you want to go into Tahrir with all the traitors and Israelis inside?" She did not want to argue with the soldiers and decided to leave. They walked her to the nearest Microbus stop and asked

Rabeea in Tahrir Square on the night of January 31st

Many people brought food to the protesters on the morning of February 3rd.
Photos, left and this page: Azza Tawfik

her to leave. She let them believe that was what she was doing, but instead she walked all the way to Mohamed Mahmoud Street and came straight back into Tahrir! Her basic instinct is so pure; she understands what is right and what is wrong, unlike many of my "educated" friends who are "convinced" that Hamas and Hezbollah have taken over Tahrir, and are asking me to leave.

Wael from Embaba: He is a 30-year-old construction worker who has never been interested in politics, demonstrations or Facebook, as he explains to me. He heard about Tahrir and the demonstrations. He was so confused at first between what he heard from his neighbors and state television and what was on Al Jazeera, that he decided to come to see for himself what was really happening in Tahrir and who was actually there. He stayed for three days and nights, then he went back home to tell his neighbors and his family that those in Tahrir are the best. The best in manners and in attitude towards each other. His words are very sincere and really touch me. He said, "I am not well educated. I left school after the fifth grade. My father died and I had to work and support my mother who was raising me and five brothers and sisters. No one explained anything to me in Tahrir, but I understood just from watching people, seeing how beautifully they dealt with each other. This is a sample of the country they want to have; a clean one with rules that we can all respect, no matter our background, and regardless of our religion and job." He simply said it! He feels it and he is proud, just like me and all of us. It feels wonderful to be among so many people whom I do not know personally but at the same time with whom I feel a strong bond.

Ahmed from Aswan: This disabled young man is in his late twenties. Ahmed has been taking part in the demonstrations in his wheelchair since January 25th. He also regularly attended previous demonstrations that opposition group Kefaya organized. I feel sorry for him on those cold nights, covered by a small blanket that he can't adjust properly with his dysfunctional arm. I ask him one morning if he needs anything. All he wants is a bottle of water and the newspaper from February 3rd.

February 9th to 11th. We are getting into day 16 now and Mubarak is still "talking"—challenging us all with his ugly speeches and perhaps banking on the fact that we may not be able to hold out. But the more he talks the more people are convinced that he has to go. Artists in Tahrir are getting creative through songs, a comic-strip exhibition along one side of the square garden, and expressive paintings. A children's painting corner is put up in later days. The solidarity in Tahrir Square shows us all that this nation is capable of building an organized country. Everything in Tahrir is organized by committees: ten toilets were built by volunteer plumbers, there are water supplies, food supplies, a group of cleaners, garbage areas, sleeping areas, places to make speeches with clear rules for participation, a photo collection area, medical support points, clinics for those requiring more than normal first-aid help, and so on.

This weekend the revolution becomes a very different experience for me. Egyptian friends are arriving from all around the world. Two of my friends left their children with their husbands and have come all the way from Canada, the United Arab Emirates and the UK to participate in the protests on Friday the 11th. More friends have come from Alexandria. Some of us go and join the sit-ins taking place in front of Parliament and in front of the presidential palace in Heliopolis. It is time for him to go.

EGYPTIANS THEMSELVES HAD TO CHANGE BEFORE THEY COULD REVOLT

Amr Waked

Amr Waked, 39, is best known to international audiences for his role with George Clooney in the 2005 feature film, Syriana. *He is renowned in Egypt as a film, television and stage actor. Mr. Waked knew that fame could make him a prime target for security forces on Tahrir Square and he had a comfortable life under President Mubarak, but he felt driven to take to the streets. While he felt it was inappropriate that fans came up to him to ask for his photograph on the square, the fact that he was so well-known served as a boost to demonstrators' morale.*

~

W hen the events started in Tunisia, I was naturally worried. If the same thing happened in Egypt it would be a complete mess: bloodshed, destruction, and chaos from which Egypt would not recover. My view was that the Tunisian population is generally cultured, educated and non-violent, yet some elements of the Egyptian population are not as cultured and are capable of violence. I was afraid this would be disastrous for Egypt. I am one of those who have had a good deal of success in Mubarak's era, so I do not have much to complain about. But I was concerned for other people, whom I knew had difficult lives. We lacked basic human rights here. I had issues with the way we were being treated as Egyptians but I was quite afraid of criticizing the regime because I am a reasonably well-known man.

So it would be very easy to arrest me or bring me in—fame means my voice is heard, so I could face worse punishment, or revenge.

I make good money. My wife and I had just had a child. So, like many others, it was easy to think, why change things? There was stability under Mubarak. I felt secure. Personally I did not have any problems and my future was looking pretty good. It's easy to tranquilize yourself with these thoughts; you even feel that you're right. But it was specifically because I had had a child recently that I needed to go against these thoughts. Maybe it was okay for me to accept the situation for myself, but I could not accept it for my son. It was my absolute responsibility to change my thinking. But still I searched for excuses to leave things as they were. Egypt was not as bad as Tunisia, which had far fewer freedoms. Deposed president Zine al-Abidine Ben Ali and his family had owned everything which was not the case in Egypt. I thought, let us try to fix things peacefully and quietly. I had great faith that revolution starts inside you and that Egyptians themselves had to change before they could revolt. For you to carry out a revolution without it turning bloody, violent and destructive, you must have a basic understanding of demonstrations and how they are carried out in a civilized manner. You must understand how to demonstrate peacefully, ask for your rights, increase your numbers until your voices are heard and ultimately your demands are met.

I started posting notes on Facebook that it is not power that controls or rules us, but all the components of a culture. I gave the example of the Moguls, who were at the time the fiercest army on Earth, unstoppable, going through country after country and razing whole cities to the ground. But then they were stopped by Islam. They didn't fight the people in this region because what stopped them was the culture of this region. I posted another note on Facebook about how bad it was that the regime was so corrupt, but that it was also lamentable that the citizens themselves were corrupted. If we were going to demand that the regime cease to be corrupt, we ourselves had to come clean.

On January 24th, I posted a note saying that we had every right to demonstrate and pressure the regime into giving us our rights. I went to the first demonstrations on Tuesday the 25th. My brother was going to go demonstrate from Shubra [a working-class district in northern Cairo] and I decided to go with him. We spent maybe two hours demonstrating that night. We started with 30 or 40 demonstrators, but people kept joining us until we were 700- or 800-strong and then the security forces chased us and we started dispersing. Naturally when they run at you with their sticks, you run away; then they started coming at us from side streets, so we dispersed. Then we heard that there was a major demonstration going on in Tahrir Square. So I got in a cab and two people I did not know got in the car with me. My brother was supposed to get into a car with some other people, but I found out that he had been arrested by the State Security forces. I also heard that they were looking for me to arrest me, so I was relieved I had left before they got me.

The phone call about my brother's arrest scared me, as did knowing that the State Security was looking for me. But as I approached Tahrir, nobody stopped me, and I became less afraid. Tons of people were in the square. I had not imagined at all that there would be this number here. It must have been tens of thousands. When people arrived and found it to be quite safe, they called others and told them to join. So the numbers were increasing all the time. We heard that there was some violence earlier in the day but that had all ended by the time I got there. The crowds kept on increasing. I was chanting "Down With Hosni Mubarak!" and "The People Want to Topple the Regime!" For me, the latter was the strongest chant of all. To think that a short time before, it mattered little what the people wanted, and now they were demanding the removal of the regime. I was chanting with the demonstrations but I was also very worried about my brother.

I called a relative of ours who worked in State Security and told him my brother Mohamed had been arrested. I was surprised that instead of offering to help get him released, he started lecturing me on how demonstrating was a stupid idea and why were we demonstrating anyway. This man is a close relative, but he said *I will see, we will try, I can't release him, this is a political decision* and things like that. I really didn't like what I was hearing and this made me more keen to continue protesting in Tahrir.

But you know what got me really angry? I was thinking, what

has my brother actually done? What crime did he commit? What did he do to be arrested? Was he not just expressing an opinion? He just had an opinion he wanted to voice! How could there be a law preventing people from thinking things, or saying them? Especially since the government had been saying for several years now that there was complete freedom of speech and expression. It is terrible that they would first give us an impression of freedom, and then when we spoke out, they would arrest us. To say that it is legal and then punish you anyway, that's a bit much. The next morning there was a ridiculous double-headline in the newspaper, on the same line and in the same font: "PM NAZIF GUARANTEES CITIZENS' RIGHT TO PEACEFUL DEMONSTRATION; MINISTER ADLY: 500 ARRESTED DURING YESTERDAY'S DEMONSTRATIONS"—in the same paper! The prime minister was guaranteeing the right of the people to demonstrate and the minister of the interior was announcing he had arrested 500 demonstrators.

Until this moment, I had no idea how much trouble I was getting myself into. I had written a note on Facebook and gone and joined a demonstration, that was all. By the time I got home, though, nearly 20,000 people had read it. It had been copied and posted on to lots of other websites, including Egyptian news website masrawy.com. My posting urged people to take to the streets and join the demonstrations. A YouTube video was also going around with me yelling "Down With Hosni Mubarak!" and "Down With the National Democratic Party!" and this video already had 250,000 views. So the State Security would screw me, no two ways about it, as though I were the one who started it all! I mean, with 250,000 views, even if a quarter of those viewers actually went to the square, that's 60,000 people! I was really scared. I thought immediately: ship the wife and kid off to Paris. My wife is French and they had been booked to travel anyway within a few days because my son needed medical attention. I brought their flight forward and flew them out immediately.

On Wednesday and Thursday (the 26th and 27th), I stayed at home; not much was going on. Thursday morning, my brother was released and on Thursday night I decided I would go to the demonstration that was leaving from Mustafa Mahmoud Mosque after Friday prayers. Friday morning, on January the 28th, I was interviewed by Al Jazeera English about all that was going on. I left their offices and went straight to the mosque, and went from there to the battle between demonstrators and security forces at Galaa Bridge, then the battle at Qasr el-Nil, then back again to Galaa Bridge then Qasr el-Nil again, then Qasr el-Nil for a third time.

This was Friday of Rage. During these battles I was close to death several times. I saw a man shot straight in the face with a shotgun. Straight in the face. We had been trying to get on top of one of the Central Security Forces (CSF) vehicles to empty it of policemen. The hatch opened up and a policeman emerged and shot the nearest person straight in the face. I scrambled down the hood of the vehicle and prayed he would not see me. They drove over people and sprayed us with water cannons while we were praying. They don't spray water just to annoy people, but because it interacts with the tear gas and screws up any exposed skin. It was real torture, just completely criminal what they were doing. The body entrusted with protecting the law was punishing the people it should have been protecting.

I flipped at this point, 180 degrees. Until that day, my demands were that the president should not be in power for more than two terms, that we dismantle the parliament and the senate, that all political prisoners be released, that we should have some political freedoms and that we free the various syndicates from the National Democratic Party cronies who were heading them. After what happened to us on the 28th, my request became much simpler: I wanted Mubarak to go. Absolutely with no discussion. Just leave. Anything else we were discussing or demanding could wait. I was emotionally devastated; I saw many people dead or dying, many. I don't know if all of them died or just some or what, they were people being carried out with wounds and bleeding and beaten, just too much to bear.

I tried as much as possible to get on the media and respond to the vicious media war being launched by the regime through the state-owned television. They were saying we were Hezbollah financed, or that this was the Muslim Brotherhood's revolution. I did my best to respond to these stupid allegations, because I was there in the square. Throughout the week, all kinds of accusations were being made: that people were paying us 50 euros (around US$65), or that they were giving us KFC meals to stay in the square, and other mindless drivel.

The first speech by the president, broadcast late on Friday night, was unbelievable. He said we must choose between security and chaos; to me this was the strongest reason why he had to go. I mean how can a president give his people this choice: either I stay and you have security, or I go but I leave you with chaos? If these are our options, then you *must* go. This is not your ranch, you are not our father, and we are not your children. I could not imagine that there was this level of arrogance, of complete tyranny, that he was giving us these choices. It felt almost as if the speeches were being written with the intent of angering people. I couldn't imagine what he was trying to do. The speeches were increasingly provocative, designed it seemed to raise the level of anger, not control it. I still can't understand it.

It was obvious how he could be such a tyrant. This man is reputed to have a personal fortune worth 50 per cent of Egypt's national debt. Half! He could reduce our debt by 50 per cent from his own personal wealth! You have to expect anything from a man that corrupt. There are forty million people living on less than a dollar a day. So even if all the numbers quoted regarding his wealth are outrageously high, and even if he "only" has a few million dollars and not the reputed tens of millions, that is still way, way, way too much. You cannot be president of this country.

So after the million-man march on Tuesday, February 1st, I believed that the revolution was growing strong and would be successful. I met one guy who told me he was a doctor; I mean he holds a degree in medicine and, unable to find a position with a decent salary, works as a tuk-tuk (motor rickshaw) driver! One of the most wonderful things for me was how we turned out to be a truly united people. Although the Coptic Church asked its adherents not to take part in the demonstrations a few days before the 25th, there were many Christians amongst us every day. Even when my brother was arrested on the very first day, he said that there was a large number of Christians arrested with him. He said the place they were held at was housing maybe 250 or 300

Amr Waked (right) gives an impromptu interview in Tahrir Square, in front of stones collected for defending the square against security forces

Tabrir Square

people and a good 50 to 60 of these were Christian. Also, Cairo was without any police presence for days, and nobody attacked any mosques or churches. And now the information coming out is that the Saints' Church attack a couple of months ago may actually have been planned by the State Security to keep people busy with sectarian issues rather than think about copying what was happening in Tunisia. If this was their doing, it was such a cheap act: raise the tension between Muslims and Christians and then the government comes in as the peacemaker, rather than have both Muslims and Christians revolting against the regime.

After that Tuesday, I was in the square every day. One day, as I was going home, a man came up to me in the street and said he had a favor to ask. He explained that his brother was a police officer and it was getting late and he didn't want to risk being on the street alone or going through the checkpoints set up by the public committees because police officers were getting very bad treatment when caught. I took him to my house and let him spend the night there and then early the next morning I took him home. He told me that on the 28th, police officers were not receiving orders for the last one and a half hours, when things got very violent. He told me that every officer made his own decisions at that point; some ran away, others used live ammunition on the protesters. He said some of the leadership had given orders earlier in the day to use live ammunition if things got out of hand, but that many officers preferred to run away rather than use their weapons on the demonstrators. But some did not. One can argue that the rubber bullets, the tear gas, the water cannons are somewhat understandable, but live ammunition is just something else altogether.

He seemed scared. That night he spent at my house, I was thinking of the depth and impact of what we had achieved, and of the police's precarious role. I thought one way forward would be for the police to change their uniform, to transform their look completely, maybe wear blue instead of black or something. A change of behavior, I felt, should come with a change in look, because the uniform we had been used to for decades was associated in our minds with their attitudes towards us. They should get retrained and re-introduced to society in a totally new way. And the events of January the 28ᵗʰ should be taught in the Police Academy as a day of great failure on the part of the Egyptian police force. Also, perhaps we should abolish the Ministry of Interior altogether and have it function as a department under the Ministry of Defence, which would handle internal security as well as external defence. The hero now in the eyes of the Egyptians is the army soldier, and we should take advantage of this. I believe that if an old blue box [police truck] were to go today into any area to make an arrest, the policemen would get beaten up, even if they were going after a real criminal. This is a big problem, and it needs an immediate and effective solution. At the same time, the police officers and policemen who are just starting to go back on the street to try and do their jobs are afraid. They need to be wary of the general public; the relationship is so poor. All the police forces need to receive rehabilitation and there needs to be a new deal between the people and the police. We need to move towards the idea that our security forces including the police work for us, the people, to protect *us*. It cannot be that we fear them, or that they fear us! The idea that the police can physically abuse someone or beat them up because of something they think or say, is unacceptable. If we achieve nothing else, and this is our only achievement from this revolution, that is already huge.

As the days went on, I started becoming upset with people who were saying we hadn't achieved anything. We had achieved a lot; some of the biggest symbols of the corrupt and despotic regime were falling one by one and that alone was a sign and lesson for the people coming into power: *Do not be corrupt*. The other thing I was thinking during these days was that we could not eradicate all corruption; that would be like eradicating Egypt. A man who made 200 Egyptian pounds (about US$40) a month and who then took bribes here and there to add another 200 pounds to his income—you could not call him corrupt. He was just trying to survive and this was how you survived in a corrupt system. But some people were robbing the country blind and they should be tried and sentenced. Perhaps there needs to be a cut-off amount, below which the act of accepting the bribe can be considered survival, and above which that person is legally corrupt and must be tried and sentenced.

Of course, throughout this period, my wife was giving me a hard time from France. She would call and cry. She kept insisting that I must leave and come to her and that I had responsibilities towards her and our son, and I explained that I could not simply get on a plane like, say, Ezz. [Ahmed Ezz is a steel magnate and monopolist billionaire businessman close to Mubarak's regime, currently going through legal proceedings for corruption.] What kind of an Egyptian would I be if I did this? I mean how could I be the same person who on the 23rd was urging people out onto the streets and then a week later I'm on a plane out? Or maybe she thought I should cheer them from abroad, like Mohamed ElBaradei, the Nobel Laureate and former UN nuclear watchdog chief, who opposed Mubarak. I am really angry with people saying it was ElBaradei who planned and carried out the revolution. That is unfair to all Egyptians. He has some followers but nowhere near enough to spark or grow the revolution to the size it reached.

I have a friend who lives on a very high floor overlooking the square so I went up to his house many times just to take a look at what it was like and took many photos. It was an amazing sight from up there. I did not spend nights at the square; I did not see a need for it, and there was hardly any space to sleep. People were daily inventing new spaces to sleep in the square. I would certainly have stayed if there were a need for it. One of the things that I believe my presence did, was to give a sense of security to some extent to the people in the square. I think there was a sense that, if they were going to bust someone, they would target famous demonstrators first.

But this famous person thing also got on my nerves several times. I remember on the Day of the Camel [when security forces and hired men on camelback used whips and other weapons to attack the demonstrators in the square] someone came up to me asking for a photo! I could not believe it. People were being killed at the other end of the square, and this guy was asking to get a photo taken with me. *Insane!* Someone is being carried half dead right in front of us, bleeding from three different places and this guy wants a photo taken! What the hell is wrong with these people? And even on the calmer days, when there was no danger, I was there to demonstrate, not have my photo taken. The thing is, you can never get done with the photos, because as soon as one person gets it, a whole queue lines up and in the end someone gets angry at you for not getting their picture taken with you, so it's a no win situation. You just have to say no and stay focused. So I did not stay in one place too long, because a crowd would form and it was uncomfortable.

Nevertheless, they were great days. I felt at the time that we were either going to come out of this victorious, or we would all be arrested and completely screwed. These were the only options. Either we win, or we will all be arrested and tortured. This meant that it had become a war. A war between those who wanted Mubarak to stay, supporting fear and humiliation, and those who wanted him gone, supporting dignity and freedom. The other thing I learned from being in Tahrir is that being brave is not that difficult; fear is the problem. I mean if I had stayed home and watched the scenes on television, I would never have gone down to the square. But being there in the square made me feel safe, although there was a lot of danger. I knew we were ten times as many people as the police. Nobody can stop all of this, there are too many of us, you cannot arrest a million people.

By Tuesday, my wife had calmed down but then on Wednesday, the Day of the Camel, she completely lost it. She was screaming at me to leave the square and leave the country and join her, but I couldn't do it. I knew we were getting close to the end, although on some days I was sure he would last for another month or two. So much so that I thought maybe I should travel to see my family and come back; but then my decision was to stay. I couldn't just leave. Meanwhile, back at work business suffered for myself and many others. But I did not care; I wanted him gone.

I loved how the demonstrations were getting strategic in their approach. We crowded the police out of the square, then we blocked the parliament, then we penned them in at the television station. Next, we were headed to the palace.

WE ARE JUST NORMAL UNDERPAID, BADLY TREATED GOVERNMENT EMPLOYEES

Ahmed S. & Ahmed M.

Ahmed S. and Ahmed M., both 28, were on duty during the 18-day revolts. Their last names are withheld on their request. While the army is generally well-liked and respected in Egypt — soldiers are often perceived as heroes, following the country's military success against Israel in the Sinai in 1973 — for Egypt's police force, it is a different story. They are largely seen as a mere extension of Mubarak's security apparatus. The police used tough tactics, including tear gas, rubber and live ammunition to put down the demonstrators. Long seen as corrupt, the police lost its legitimacy during the 18-day revolution. One contributor to this book even suggested that, short of a complete overhaul and extensive soul-searching, the police force would never earn the respect of the Egyptian people again. These are two young policemen who were caught in the middle of a struggle with little instruction from their superiors.

~

The evening before Tuesday, January the 25th, we were told that there would be a demonstration. We were told to exercise extreme self-control. *They may swear at you. Keep quiet. They may get angry with you. Keep quiet. Nobody was to "deal" with them at all. Whatever happens let them walk freely and go wherever they want.* Those were the instructions. Let them vent their anger. No contact with the people at all. And on Tuesday, about

15,000 people started converging on Tahrir and we followed our instructions; nobody from the police side so much as talked to them. We let them get to Tahrir in peace. At midnight, the people in Tahrir said they would spend the night. Our superiors said they couldn't spend the night, and we were ordered to disperse the demonstration. Just a demonstration, is what we were told. So the riot-control police started dealing with them in the normal way, tear gas, water cannons and within 28 minutes, it was all dispersed. No more demonstrators.

That night we arrested maybe 500 people. They were taken to the Central Security camps and we began to question them. We split them into three or four groups, students, journalists and media, activists known to us from before and people who were just there to join in. We kept most of them for two days and then on Thursday night we released more than 90 per cent of them. That was stupid, of course. To keep someone locked up for 48 hours and then release them a day before a big demonstration, it was just stupid. Either release them immediately on Tuesday or Wednesday morning before they get too angry, or keep them locked up till after the big Friday demonstrations. I was one of the officers who was taking locked-up demonstrators from the camps and releasing them onto the streets. We just took them in cars and let them go anywhere. Most of them were a bit dazed and in shock over being locked up for two days, then suddenly released.

Then on Thursday night our superiors started talking to us about how we would deal with the expected Friday of Rage. While nothing much was happening between Tuesday and Friday, it was clear that there were bigger preparations for Friday. But still the thinking in the police force was the same: just more demonstrations. The decision was made by the superiors not to allow large groups to link up to form a mass demonstration. The decision was to disperse them as early as possible when they were still in small groups. When my colleagues and I asked how, they told us to use tear gas and water cannons. Now the problem is that tear gas chokes people and can work for a few hundred, but you cannot choke thousands or millions. It will not have the same impact; it will only make people angrier.

At the same time, we were ordered not to take any live

ammunition. All live ammunition was taken from the officers and soldiers. The instructions to us were very clear and strict: you will only use tear gas and rubber bullets. Do you know what rubber bullets are? They hurt a little, like a bee sting or something. Even if I shoot you at close range, it will make a bruise and it will hurt, of course, but there is no way you can kill someone, even at very close range. So anything you hear about people dying from rubber bullets is just a lie. You cannot kill someone with a rubber bullet. Now, apart from the official guns and rifles we have as a police force, every officer also has what we call 'tasleeh shakhsy' or personal arms. This is my own gun, which I take home with me every night. I know many officers who took these with them despite orders not to have live ammunition with us on Friday, and this is maybe where some of the live ammunition came from.

On Friday morning, the 28th—what later became Friday of Rage—I was in Ramses Street, near al-Fath Mosque. The demonstrators were approaching our blockade and they were many. We had maybe 90-100 soldiers and ten officers and there must have been more than 5,000 protesters. It was clear we could not repel them.

After a short while, we ran out of tear gas and our water tanks were empty and they rushed us. One of the demonstrators took a tear gas canister that was still active and threw it into one of our armored vehicles, almost killing everyone inside; thank God, they got out of the vehicle in time. All the officers ran away after that, because it was clear the crowd would get violent. Of course this was the time when one of the policemen who was driving the water cannon vehicle panicked and drove off like a maniac and hit some people or ran them over, I'm not sure. I had two options; stay and use my personal gun and maybe kill two or three before they killed me, or run away. So I ran away instead of having the guilt of killing someone on my conscience. We contacted our superiors and they told us to return to the camps, because there was nothing we could do anymore. I went back to my police station and met with Ahmed M. —*Ahmed S.*

We were sitting in the police station, my colleagues and I, watching television to see what was going on. Everything was still okay, when suddenly we saw on Al Jazeera that our police station was under attack and that people had set fire to it! This was half an hour *before* anybody attacked our police station. They had the news before it happened! When we saw this news we went outside to get people to move on from the front of the station, telling them "Not here, not here, move on."

Most people were responsive and just moved on with the demonstrators on their way to Tahrir, but five or maybe six guys insisted that they wanted to get inside the police station. They were trying to get people from the crowds of demonstrators to help them rush the police station. For maybe 10 or 15 minutes, nobody was responding, so they did something very strange, but it worked. They ran towards the entrance of the police station and then one of them fell to the ground and the others started yelling, "These bastards have shot him! The policemen shot him!" It was a complete theatrical piece. Nobody had fired a single shot.

But of course some of the demonstrators, already angry from the tear-gassing and the water cannons, started joining this group. At this point one of my police officer colleagues lost his cool. Hundreds of people were running towards the police station. My colleague fired warning shots into the air. I think he panicked at the sight of the crowds running towards us. This made the demonstrators even angrier. So we went inside and quickly locked the gates from the inside as the demonstrators tried to break in. There was a lot of panic. There were six or seven officers and maybe 20 ordinary police and other employees. We could not get through to our superiors. The mobile networks were shut down; our walkie-talkies had lost power. They have a battery life of five or six hours, and we had been on the street since 5 or 6am, so we had no method of communication. We tried the landlines, but most of the senior officers were on the street dealing with demonstrations. We decided that our main job was to try to protect the police station from attack. From the inside we saw and heard demonstrators destroying police cars and one or more were set on fire. Then they started trying to storm the building by breaking down the gates. A shot was fired from outside through the gates and killed one policeman which caused a bigger panic. We put all of our weapons in the armory. We did not want to use live ammunition against the demonstrators and at the same time we did not want them to get their hands on the guns and rifles. In my police station we have 288 pieces, of which 130 are automatic. We could have dealt with the demonstrators, but we would have killed many. So we decided not to deal with them and flee instead, to avoid a catastrophe. The armory has a heavy metal door and is well-secured. With all of our weapons inside, we ran upstairs onto the roof. At this time, another group of people started lighting up natural gas tanks, the type used for home cooking, and throwing them at the police station. The building caught fire. We heard the people downstairs breaking down the gates and coming in. They started trashing the police station until they discovered the armory and broke down the metal door, I don't know how, because it is a really thick and heavy door. Then we heard gunshots, so we knew that they had broken into the holding areas of the guns. We heard people running up the stairs screaming, "They must be upstairs!"

Two of my colleagues and I jumped from the roof of the police station onto the roof of the adjacent building and ran down the stairs and knocked on the door of an old lady we knew from the neighborhood. She took us in but she was hysterical and in tears. She kept screaming, "Why are they doing this? Why are they burning the police station? What are all these gunshots I am hearing? What is happening?" We tried to calm her down and asking her to keep her voice down so people outside would not discover we were in her house. We stayed there for maybe two hours until someone outside somehow found out that we were inside and they started calling people off the street to come into the building and find us. All the residents of the building were evacuating. So the lady, God bless her, gave us some clothes to be able to mingle with the residents. She gave me a pair of pyjamas and gave the other two *galabeyas* [traditional Egyptian garments for men] and thank God we were able to escape unharmed within the throng of residents running down the stairs and out onto the street. One of the police officers who was with me walked to his house nearby. I live at the other end of town. When I looked in front of the police station, I found my car was not there, it turned out it had been stolen. I still haven't recovered it.

I met some of the area's residents on the street. They knew me from their dealings with the police station. I had been stationed there for almost seven years, so I had many acquaintances in the neighborhood. They were a bunch of Christian guys and they took me to their home and fed me and asked me to stay for the night but I didn't want to. I ate and called my parents and watched some television. I found out that 24 other police stations had been attacked at almost the same time as ours, which made me feel it was a planned attack. I left an hour or so later and went to another police officer's house nearby and spent the night there. When I went back to my police station the next day, it was a terrible sight, all burned and all the glass broken; they even stole the furniture from inside. It made me very sad.

I went home again hoping to receive some instructions from our superiors but we did not receive any. I did not know what to do. The police station was burned; there was news of shooting at the Ministry of Interior so I could not go there. Also there was news of shooting at the Cairo Police Headquarters, so I could not go there either. So I stayed at home during the day and in the evening I joined the neighborhood watch around our area. I was born and raised in the neighborhood, so the people there all knew me well and they knew I was a police officer, so they were asking me for advice on how to man the barricades and how to search people and search cars.

I just carried on like this until Monday when we received instructions to get back on the street and go to our police stations and try and find a suitable location nearby to start working from again. We found a school quite close to the station and started meeting there, my colleagues and I. Of course we were not in uniform because we did not want any confrontations with the public. At first, we had nothing to do, but then word got out that we were stationed there and people started coming to us. They came with a lot of stolen goods, weapons that were stolen from the armory and criminals they had caught themselves. We set up a makeshift police station and started trying to get work done.

I think one of the big problems is that people don't understand that we are just normal underpaid, badly treated government employees like everyone else. I work 12 hours a day, seven days a week. I have no weekends and only 15 days of leave per year. I have been in service for more than seven years, but my salary is 1,200 Egyptian pounds a month (around US$210). This is all-inclusive and we quite frequently get pay deductions of five or 10 days, so sometimes I make even less. When we perform extra paid duties, such as guarding an embassy or a bank or securing a motorcade, we should get paid around US$10 per hour, but the Ministry keeps 60 per cent of this, and the Headquarters gets another 25 per cent or more and I end up making maybe 10 or 15 per cent of what is actually paid. On a very good month, I might make an extra 120 pounds (around US$20). If I did not live with my parents or if I were married, I would not be able to survive.

—*Ahmed M.*

THIS WAS A QUESTION OF FAITH, AND OUR FAITH HAD BEEN CEMENTED IN FEAR

Hatem & Islam Mo'men

Hatem Mo'men is co-owner of the Mo'men fast-food chain, one of the largest in Egypt; the Planet Africa theme restaurants; and the Three Chefs Frozen Foods Factory. Despite being a successful businessman under the Mubarak regime, Mr. Mo'men joined the demonstrations because, as he describes, he was "sick and tired" of the lack of dignity Egyptians were suffering. Mr. Mo'men and his brother, Islam, are classic examples of how this was a multi-class uprising.

Islam Mo'men co-owns Mo'men fast-food stores with his brother Hatem. He had enough wealth that he could survive the rising food prices and endemic corruption so for him, like so many others, the protests were about Egyptians' loss of dignity and sense of freedom under Mubarak. "I had had enough of this whole idea of being driven around like goats," he said. "We were treated like sheep, led here, led there, with no say in our destinies." Mr. Mo'men was arrested, together with his wife and driver, and blindfolded during the demonstrations.

~

I was travelling for business until January 25th and, when I landed in Egypt, I went straight home and did not consider joining the demonstrations. I got a call from a friend who worked in State Security who asked me where I was. I told him I had just arrived from abroad and was at home, and then asked him how the demonstrations were going. He said everything would be "finished" that day. I told him that if things lasted until tomorrow they could escalate rapidly, and he then said that was the reason he was calling: to make sure I was at home and that if I was in Tahrir, to go home immediately because things might get rough. The instructions were to finish this thing off tonight.

On the 28th I decided that I should go. It felt like the right thing to do. I am not in any way involved in politics; I do not belong to any party or political movement. I have no shortage of money, thank God. I live well, our business is doing well, everything is fine, but I love this country and I am tired of the lack of dignity, the humiliation we feel as Egyptians. So on Friday, we went to Sultan Hassan Mosque at the end of Thawra Street in Heliopolis. As soon as prayers were done we left the mosque and went outside. We found four, maybe five guys who were there for demonstrations and we also found two Central Security formations on the opposite side. I was with my brothers, Islam and Mohamed. The officer from Central Security, who I think was a decent man, came over to us and told us to leave the area or he would have to arrest us. The place was cordoned off and he advised us to leave immediately one by one, not as a group of six or seven people.

We got into our cars and drove to Mohandiseen to Mustafa Mahmoud Mosque where we knew there would be other demonstrators; indeed, we found a large demonstration there and walked with them. I think Central Security officers were very intelligent. They allowed us to walk all the way down the wider streets of Batal Ahmed Abdel Aziz and Tahrir Street and then blocked us at the narrow entrance of the bridge, right at the end of Tahrir Street.

This is where they started hitting us with the tear gas. We had learned from the Tunisian experience, so we were well prepared with vinegar and Coke. They fired a lot of tear gas that day, and one of the canisters landed at the gas station at the end of Tahrir Street. The workers at the station had to put it out before it caught fire. Honestly I was quite afraid at that point. This was the first demonstration I had ever joined in, so I had no idea how to deal with it or what to do. But despite my fear, I was insistent that we continue, regardless of consequences. The police continued to hit us with the tear gas until I guess they ran out and then retreated to the edge of Qasr el-Nil Bridge. At the end of the bridge, they made a very strong attack, and we had to run back and got split up into several groups. Some people ran towards the Sixth of October Bridge to try and go from behind the riot control police. Others went to Sheraton Gezira area, and I was among these. We were surrounded by policemen and officers; the officers were asking us to be reasonable, explaining that they were on our side, and that they had not slept in three days and to just stay here instead of having them run around after us. At that time, a whole new and very large group of demonstrators had arrived. They had been walking from Giza in their own march and they merged with us.

A short while later, we saw three armored vehicles belonging to the army approaching and we felt a great deal of relief. If the army was taking over, we felt, we should be safe. We cheered for them, but then a short while afterwards the riot police started firing at us again using tear gas and rubber bullets. We all understood that these armored vehicles had brought more ammunition to the riot police. Up until this point all we wanted to do was to get to Tahrir. Honestly, thinking back, I don't even know why we wanted to get there, it was like a symbol or something. Added to this, their insistence on not letting us reach it made us more eager to get there, and it became the symbol of success. If we got through we made it, if we didn't then we failed.

What would we find in Tahrir when we got there? I did not know, but it was our will against theirs and we had to prevail. Whoever forces their will upon the other first will be on top forever, and whoever loses will lose forever, that is what it felt like. Anyway, they kept retreating. It was like this: we would rush them, then they would fire tear gas and we would retreat, over and over until they ran out of canisters. They would then retreat and we would move forward. We kept gaining ground until we reached the old Ministry of Foreign Affairs building, overlooking Tahrir Square. They had made like a barricade close-by and were firing their tear gas at us from behind it and at that point we started throwing stones at them.

We were very close to Tahrir and just wanted to break through this final barrier and get through. In the end we were right there, just a little distance from Tahrir. My younger brother Islam said, "I need a hundred martyrs right now. We will rush these soldiers, they may or may not kill us, but then the rest of us will get through." I raised my hand and said, "I am the first of the hundred." We immediately found not a hundred, but maybe 500 people starting to rush the barrier. We threw stones as we ran and others beat stones against the iron fences of the bridge, making a fearful and deafening noise. We must have struck fear into their hearts. The policemen fired rubber bullets insanely at this time. As we approached them, they knew we were not stopping and started getting out of the way to let us through. At least that is what we thought; it turned out they had let the first batch through and then rounded us up from behind Omar Makram Mosque to form a pincer around us. We were now surrounded from both sides. We knew that we had only two choices: either get through or die. Personally, I felt I would never again have my will broken. I was getting through, or dying there.

At this time, we saw the National Democratic Party (NDP) Headquarters building being set on fire. We all knew at the same time that NDP officials were setting fire to it themselves because there must have been countless incriminating documents and evidence inside it. It was a very organized fire, first one floor then the next. It was not a random fire, as you would expect if demonstrators had started it. It seemed from the outside that they were going into each room and setting documents on fire, or something like that. We got through to Tahrir by rushing at the riot-control police surrounding us. Seeing the NDP building set on fire gave us renewed energy. We found a strange vehicle firing green-blue gas at people and driving through the crowds insanely. It drove over a man right in front of my eyes; there was nothing left of him except his shoe. The rest of his body was in pieces. Several guys jumped onto the car and grabbed the policeman who was driving it and pulled him out. We found tonnes of weapons in the truck. There was a big argument on what to do with these weapons. In the end the older people, and I among them, convinced the younger crowd it would be best if we threw all the weapons in the Nile, which we did.

Later that night, I regretted that decision. That night, the police were using live ammunition against us. Anyway, I will come to that later. At that time they had stopped hitting us with the tear gas, so we figured they must have run out of canisters again. We rested for a little while. There were many injured people and an ambulance came through and we let it through thinking they were there to get the injured people, but they didn't take anybody and a few minutes later the ambulance was gone. The police started firing again, so that ambulance must have been carrying ammunition, can you imagine? When the next ambulance came through, we stopped it and checked it and found weapons and gas canisters inside. Insane!

I remember at that time, we were organized in a very random way. Nobody was managing us, but some were hitting iron fences to make noise, others were breaking up the sidewalk for stones, others were carrying the stones and still others were throwing the stones. Automatically and without previous organization, if anyone got tired throwing, he would be replaced and so on. Random but organized. I was throwing stones and looked behind me to find a guy with a bullet in his belly. We stopped throwing to carry him towards the back but he insisted he was fine and that we should leave him and carry on. He was dead the next time I looked in his direction.

In a short while, we had taken over the entire square. The police were on the outskirts still hitting us with tear gas. Some officers were firing shotguns from atop the American University in Cairo building. There were also snipers firing at anyone who got close to the Ministry of Interior. Nonetheless, things were relatively stable, and I thought I should try and reach my wife, just to tell her I was still alive. When I had left my house, I was uncertain whether I would go back. I gave her my credit cards and my PIN codes—for the first time in my life. I tried finding a phone; the cell phones were out because the government had switched all three networks off to stop people communicating. After looking for a while, I found a man who had extended a cord from inside his house and was letting people call from his home phone. He totally refused payment. He would not take a penny from anyone. I called my wife and told her I was okay. Right down the street, I found a fruit stand and he had some bananas left. I bought the whole lot and took them back to the square. As I walked back to the square, I found a small group of Central Security soldiers. I started talking to them very quietly, "How could you do this to us? We are Egyptians just like you." They said they were just following orders and had no choice but to follow them. They said they did not want to attack or hit us, but those were their orders. One of them was especially scared and told me he was afraid that people might kill him if they saw him in uniform. I gave him a t-shirt, an undershirt I was wearing, so he could use it instead of his uniform.

When I got back into the square, around 2am, I was amazed that they had already set up a field hospital and things were getting organized very quickly in order to tend to the injured. Then someone said that the Tahrir Telephone Exchange was working, so I thought I should call my family again. I went and queued up, and of course there was a long queue waiting to make phone calls. Standing in the queue an old woman, maybe 70 years old, and she gave me a number on a piece of paper and asked me to call it. I dialled the number for her; she took the phone from me and said, "Yes, this is Om Ahmed, I am okay," and hung up. I told her she should go home, it was very late, she was better off at home. She said, "No. This is the first time I say NO in my life. I will die here, I am never leaving Tahrir. This is my home now."

While I was talking to my wife the second time, she told me that there was news on television that the Egyptian Museum was being robbed. I quickly ran towards the museum and asked people to come with me and many joined immediately. We arrived and formed three lines in front of the museum's main gate, and three more in front of the back entrance and I called one of the demonstrators off the street and told him to run quickly to the television building and ask the army to send a tank or armored vehicle or something to protect the museum. We stayed there protecting the building until a short while later an army tank with some soldiers came and parked at the front entrance of the museum. We felt better that the museum was now protected. This is our history and we cannot allow it to be robbed during the chaos. Unfortunately, before we had arrived, the gift shop had been broken into, but none of the items stolen were of any archaeological value, just copies. After the incident at the museum there was a lot of talk among the people in the square that we should move on and try to take the Parliament building. I was against this. I thought that we had freed Tahrir Square and we should stay and protect it. Just now as I am thinking, I had never before thought of the square's name as having any meaning, but the name now strikes me: Tahrir Square, Liberation Square. We liberated Tahrir Square.

The next morning, people were insistent that they should take over the Ministry of Interior building. The older demonstrators tried to convince them that this was a bad idea, but they would not listen. There was a lot of anger and hatred towards this ministry. They were not being rash or impulsive, but there was a lot of anger. A group of five would go and return with two dead, then ten would go and come back with three dead.

There is something I want to mention for history to remember. This will not be mentioned anywhere else, because only an eyewitness can tell this story, and I was there myself. When the first tanks came into Tahrir, we did not know whether we could trust the army. We stood in front of the tank, but the soldier driving it was inept and he drove over one of the demonstrators by mistake. The demonstrator who was crushed had friends with him, and one of them climbed onto the tank and slit the throat of the driver. He actually slit his throat. The commander ran over, saw the crushed demonstrator and saw the slaughtered tank driver and did not utter a word. He understood what had happened and did not take any action.

The tanks started coming into the square one by one. We were letting them through and to me this meant that we, the people, were giving the army the right to enter the square. Every tank had at least thirty, maybe forty demonstrators on board. They were allowed in, but on our terms, and if a tank driver tried to get into the square too quickly, we would climb onto his tank and stop him until we were ready to let him through. It was we, the people, who

The revolution went on through the night

gave the army its legitimacy. We removed any legitimacy from the previous government when we demonstrated. We removed the police's legitimacy when we entered Tahrir Square and we gave the army its legitimacy when we let them into Tahrir.

The first days passed and we became confident that the army was trustworthy. Sunday and Monday nothing much happened, we had of course some food shortages, but apart from that everything was quite stable and secure. By Monday, it was clear the government was trying another tactic. It seemed they were sending people into the square to try and sway people's minds. We found people coming to us and saying, "What more do you want, we have achieved a lot, let everyone go back to work, you have achieved a lot already," and things like that. Of course, my strong belief is that these people were sent by the government to try and sway people's opinions.

By Tuesday morning, the scene was changing in Tahrir. Many people were there to take a look or to appear on television, and people were carrying signs and posters just to get on television. I was happy with the numbers, but I didn't like the lack of conviction and belief. The one thing that was very obvious, also, was the behavior of the people. Manners were very evident. Sheikh Safwat Hegazy was making a speech and he said, "Muslims and Christians are all one. We are all Egyptians." A bearded Muslim man was chanting behind him and I videotaped him and asked if he would mind if I put the video on YouTube. He said he did not mind at all. He had just seen an even more wonderful sight back in Sahel, where he lived. The sunnis (relatively strict Muslims) were guarding the local church from harm. And this was true; there was no sectarian trouble in Egypt.

We were without any police presence in the streets for three days. Not one window was broken in a single church or mosque. Would that time not have been a perfect opportunity? If the Muslims and Christians of Egypt really hated each other, this would have been a perfect chance to attack mosques and churches, but not a stone was thrown at any place of worship. We cleaned the streets together with Christians and the behavior was excellent between everyone, rich, poor, Christian, Muslim, men, women, everybody. I was very impressed with everybody's attitude. There were attractive girls amongst us, dressed very nicely, and they faced no harassment. No one bothered any of the girls; if your wife or daughter or sister were walking, a hundred men would look out for her, making sure she was not bothered in any way.

Tuesday, for me, was the greatest day of treachery. If this man [Mubarak] cared about this country, he would have resigned that day. It was clear that the most Egyptians had united behind one goal. He delivered his "great" speech, saying he wanted to die in Egypt and all of that. He worked on our emotions and our sentiments. And we as Egyptians must be the most sentimental people in the world. I tried to talk to people, telling them that he had said nothing of significance; he was just playing the emotional card. He had given us nothing. Nothing had changed. Some people listened but others started leaving Tahrir. I remember that day I went to the field hospital after the speech to see if anyone needed help. When I got there people were asking if someone had a car because a young girl needed to be taken to hospital immediately. She was from Suez and had come to Cairo to join the revolution. She was diabetic and when she heard the speech, her blood sugar level shot up to 600. She was about to go into a coma. They could not treat her at the field hospital. She was shivering and shaking and I took her in my car with two doctors from the field hospital. We got her to the hospital. I went home that day and spent the night at home.

The next morning, on Wednesday the 2nd of February, I returned to the square with a heavy mix of feelings, hope and desperation. But inside me was this insistence. I had not gone to Tahrir to hear a speech, I had gone to get rid of this man. I believe I was the first to chant, "Al-Shaab Yureed Eskat el-Raees!" (The People Want to Topple the President!). Not the regime, not the system: the president himself. Once he was gone, we could talk about what else we wanted, but first the serpent's head must be removed. I wanted to see him resign and live as a normal ex-president, with one winter suit, one summer suit, a few shirts, a thick pair of pants for the winter and another lighter one for the summer, one pyjama for the summer and another for winter. He used to live at 4, Hegaz Street, he should retire and go back there and earn no more than the Mubarak pension he was giving

all retired people in Egypt [84 Egyptian pounds, about US$15].
You know, of course, I would love for all the money he stole from
this country to be returned and invested in Egypt, but even if it
doesn't, if we just succeeded in stopping the bleeding that was
happening as a result of corruption, we would find the money
pouring into the country. I just wished he could live on the
pension that he thought was adequate for all retired Egyptians.
Didn't he used to say, "Where am I supposed to find money
for all your needs?" Well, let us see where he would have found
money for himself.

In any case, when I went to the square that Wednesday, I
was trying to motivate myself. I found that the numbers had
dwindled, but I reassured myself that we were still plenty. To
anyone who tried to convince me that the speech the night before
was good, I responded that this was not about him personally,
that this was a message. Hosni might die tomorrow. I wanted
to send a message to whoever succeeds him. If we accepted that
he could stay, then the next one would receive the message that
he could rule over us in any way he wanted, and throw us a
piece of meat as though we were dogs and as if to say, "This is
enough for you," and we would just have to wait for him to die.
This was not my target at all. So with people saying it was only
six months until he left and why was that such a big problem,
I would say, all right, you might have achieved your target, so
leave the square, but do not stay here and confuse people or sway
them emotionally. I am staying because my target has not been
achieved. I worked very hard that morning to convince people
of my viewpoint.

I remember a young girl with fantastic spirit. She was
yelling, "What is the matter with you people? Have you given
up or what? We have gained nothing yet. Don't you realise that?
Nothing has been achieved." She was a pretty young girl in a
pair of jeans, but she seemed as strong as fifty men.

At around 2pm, a pro-Mubarak march was heading towards
the square. We formed a counter-demonstration and went
towards them to block them. As we neared them, they started
throwing stones at us. So we threw stones back and pushed them
back onto Abdel Moneim Riad Street. Then all at the same

time, thugs started coming at us from all directions, from Talaat Harb Street, from Bab el-Louk and from Abdel Moneim Riad Square. They were throwing ball bearings and stones at us and were increasing in numbers rapidly. We rushed back towards the first tank and tried to get the army officer on that tank to help us. His name was Maged. These thugs were coming at us. We begged him to help us in any way at all. He blew his whistle to attract his superior's attention, but apparently he could not or would not hear him. He blew his whistle again, but was ignored. My brother Islam went to him and begged him for help. But his commander did not respond to his whistling. A man draped in the Egyptian flag went up onto the tank; he kissed the officer's head, asking him to please do something to help us. He implored him: "We are one, the army and these demonstrators are one, we are all Egyptians. We are the same people!" The officer grabbed the flag and kissed it, went on his knees and kissed the man's foot, and then stood up and without permission from his commander raised his pistol into the air and fired warning shots into the air. When the chamber emptied, he put another one in and emptied that one into the air too. The thugs backed off at the sound of live bullets and we immediately started setting up blockades. The officer broke into tears at that point and several demonstrators went up to him to calm him down.

I went to the front lines and started throwing stones at the thugs to drive them further back. Then there was a cry from our crowd saying that the thugs were coming from another direction, so we went over and threw stones at them. One of the thugs got onto the roof of a building and started throwing stones at us from above. The building had scaffolding on the outside, like they were painting it or something. A young man, God bless him, climbed the scaffolding and evaded the stones that the thug was throwing at him until he got to the top of the building and stopped him. The worst fighting was at Abdel Moneim Riad Square. We hid behind one of the barricades we had put up and threw stones. I remember thinking during that time, I had been going to the gym regularly for a while and maybe God had been preparing me for this day. I threw stones until my shoulder became dislocated. I didn't know what to do.

I did not want to stop throwing but my shoulder was a mess. I had a flag wrapped around me, so I took the flag and started moving stones in it to the men who were throwing. I tied a piece of cardboard on top of my head as protection.

I want to tell you something about that Wednesday. The revolution was sparked by the first demonstration on January the 25th. This revolution could have died out a week later, on Tuesday the 1st of February, the night Mubarak made that sentimental speech that resulted in dividing the people in the street. The Muslim Brotherhood held the revolution together the following day when they repelled the thugs. I was there and I witnessed their actions. They were organized and serious, and they behaved with courage. They were right there on the front lines pushing back the thugs. Someone said something beautiful about them: "Present in the hardest of times and not requesting the bounties and spoils". We were going through the fight and there were many members of the Muslim Brotherhood in the square praying to God for help and when someone would call out, "We need more men here," four lines of Muslim Brotherhood would advance to the front lines to relieve the exhausted men. That day, I saw impressive young women, 18- to 20-year-old medical students, working in the field hospital within reach of the thugs' stones. There were so many injured people; at least three quarters of the demonstrators were injured that day.

As I was collecting stones, I saw a young man with an open wound on his forehead. He went to the field hospital, got it stitched up and came back to throw again. He suffered another cut to the head and again went to the field hospital, got it stitched and returned to throw again. The next time he went out to throw stones he got hit very badly in the nose with a large stone. I was helping him along and he was crying, so I asked him why he was crying, and he said, "I can't throw any more. Every time I try to throw a stone, my nose bleed gets worse." I tried to calm him down and said it was time for prayers, anyway, and maybe by the time we finished praying his nose would be better. As we were walking to the prayer area, he told me his only sin had been his habit of performing the early-morning prayer at the mosque. He had been taken by State Security, beaten, electrocuted in sensitive areas, hung up from a wooden plank in the ceiling and beaten again. They had done all this while saying, "You had better stop going to the mosque, you son of a this and that." He told me as we walked, "I will not be tortured again. I will not."

That day, I decided that if the revolution were to fail, I would emigrate. I would just leave the country and go live somewhere else. I would sell off my businesses and leave. But then I thought to myself, this would never happen. I would either die here or win. There was no turning back. This was a question of faith, and our faith had been cemented in fear. We were certain that if Mubarak was not removed, everyone who had set foot in Tahrir would be arrested and tortured. He would create a huge prison somewhere out in the desert and throw us all in it. This fear held our faith in place; we knew we were right, we knew we were doing the right thing, but our faith needed strengthening and our fear helped us stay strong. It had to be victory or death, no third alternative. That faith gave us so much strength. Quoting the Holy Quran: "You did not throw when you threw, it was God who threw." I swear I would see the stones I was throwing go further than I ever thought possible, across huge distances. I never imagined that this arm here could throw that far. I was throwing two or three stones at a time for my own survival.

I have a confession to make. I am not really brave. I am actually quite cowardly. I had never been in a fight. If I ever saw a fight in the street I would always walk away, and if someone in a fight pulled out a penknife, I would run. But courage is like a disease, it comes to you suddenly. All of a sudden, you are a brave man. Besides, there was no negative ending. Either victory or martyrdom.

In any case, by 2am things had calmed down relatively in the square. I was taking cover by the museum's fence and a group decided to try to get up on the bridge to remove the last of the thugs who were still sporadically throwing stones and firing guns at us. They were brave, but in my opinion they were being rash. As it happened, they were right, because they did manage to dislodge this group of thugs.

You know, on that day we caught some of those thugs. We captured them, off their horses, off their camels, and some who

Handheld devices and social media were an integral tool of the revolution

Casings from live ammunition used against the protesters

were on foot. There were two types. Some of them were paid 50 pounds (around US$9); these were smaller guys, used to add to the numbers and make a lot of noise. Others were paid 120-150 pounds (US$22-28), and these were the big guys; they were paid to beat people up and scare them into leaving the square. They were also promised a small flat and 5,000 pounds (around US$900) if they succeeded in getting us out of the square. By that time, my shoulder was really hurting, so I went to the other end of Tahrir where there were ambulances taking the injured away and tending to the wounded. I needed a sling or something to hold my shoulder in place. I found many injured people who were afraid to get into the ambulances. This was the level of mistrust, they were not sure the ambulances would take them to hospitals. These were government ambulances and people were afraid they might take them to State Security offices. I told the ambulance driver, "Some of these people would prefer to die here than get into your ambulance." Anyway, because of my shoulder, I went home that night and came back the next morning.

One of my friends called me and told me there was a man going around the square giving people fifty pounds and telling them, "Be strong brother, this is for you from the Muslim Brotherhood." I was shocked. We searched for this man until we found him. He had a bag with more than 30,000 pounds in it, in fifties, all forged, all with one serial number. If you were not well-dressed he would give you fifty pounds and if you were better dressed he would give you a hundred pounds and say, "Stay strong, we are the Muslim Brotherhood." After that Wednesday, the Day of the Camel, many of those in the square had witnessed how valiantly the Muslim Brotherhood defended the square. The rumor began spreading that the Muslim Brotherhood was taking over the revolution. Clearly this man was sent in by State Security to fuel this rumor and increase concerns in the crowd that the Muslim Brotherhood was indeed taking over the square. He eventually confessed to us that he was a State Security officer from Sharkeya and we handed him over to the army.

That day, Thursday, there was another rumor going around that the tanks were going to close in on the square to minimise the number of demonstrators. I ran to the nearest tank to make sure it could not move in and make our plot smaller. I found six rows of people lying down in front of the tank and, of course, the tank could not move at all. Others were sitting right on the chains that encircled the wheels, making it impossible for the tank to move in any direction. I had never seen such bravery. I had never imagined we could be a race of people with the ability to be so heroic in trying to achieve our goals.

That night, Mubarak came out with his speech. I felt massively depressed and demotivated. I said, "Tomorrow we go to the palace. He does not understand; we must deliver the message to his doorstep." Some 3,000 people walked out of Tahrir that night and went straight to the palace, right after the speech. The army did something that made me stop and think. Those who had gone towards the palace had arrived by around 1am. The army asked them to park their cars and let them go on by foot. The other thing I noticed was that there was something strange about the speech. Mubarak was reading off a prompter at first, then there was evidently some editing, and then he was reading from a sheet of paper. I didn't know what was going on, but it seemed to me that the speech was going from "I am leaving" to "I am not leaving; I will not accept any external pressure; and I am handing over responsibility to Omar Suleiman." This meant that the army had made a decision to rid the country of both Mubarak and Omar Suleiman, while also delivering a message to foreign powers that we would not accept any pressure from abroad. If my reading of the situation is accurate, this was a highly patriotic act. They refused foreign pressure to drop Mubarak but keep Suleiman—and in one move, they would get rid of both.

Then I heard the next announcement from the Higher Council of the Military Forces, and felt that the army was reassuring the people that even if they were to go to the palace, no force would be used against them. What we needed now was huge numbers at the palace. So I called up people still in Tahrir to urge them to come and to send as many people as possible towards the palace.

—*Hatem Mo'men*

I remember my driver asking me, "Why are you going to these demonstrations, Mr Islam? You live in a nice villa in a gated community, with a swimming pool. Your kids go to prestigious schools. What are you demonstrating for?" This was his view: that I had nothing to complain about. I told him I was doing it for my dignity, I could not accept that there was one person running the country as though we were a small corner store that he owned and ran the way he wanted to. I told him I hated the corruption that was becoming so extreme.

I was excited by what I had seen in Tahrir on the first day. I campaigned on Facebook, urging people to go to Tahrir on Friday, January 28th. I also emailed a well-known poem to my friends, which included the line: "And if you cannot bear the hardships of climbing mountains, then accept to live forever at the bottom of the slope." I have a group of friends to whom I send daily messages with a quotation from the Prophet's sayings, so I started selecting relevant quotes, such as: "If any of you sees evil being done, you have a responsibility to try and stop it." I found an old decree by Al-Azhar scholars clarifying that any Muslim who does not speak out against tyranny and injustice is not fulfilling his obligations as a Muslim. I raised the tone of my communication with people, to the extent that my older brother, Mohamed, started fearing for my safety. He told me to calm things down, saying our businesses could be affected. I knew that I was under surveillance and that my phone was tapped. I knew this, but I had had enough.

I remember on the Thursday before Friday of Rage, I attended a lecture by Dr. Mustafa Hegazy, a political thinker, and he told us we had to go through three stages for the [revolution] to succeed: mobilization, liberation, and finally, rebuilding. Dr. Mustafa said that this was our mobilization phase. If we could reach a critical mass, then we would move towards liberation. Friday, he said, would be a time to ignore one's own interests, even if there were beatings and tear gas. He then asked us who amongst us felt this was a free country, and who believed it to be under occupation. Most people said they believed Egypt was under occupation. He said that in 1919, during our revolution against the British occupation, the occupier was easily identified: he was fair-skinned and he was not Egyptian. Today, things were a lot more difficult: the occupier looked like us.

My wife worried about me, but when I told her my brothers Mohamed and Hatem would join me at the protests, this gave her some comfort. I had an Egyptian flag that I had bought before at a football game so I put that in the car with a poster I had made. I had read on Facebook that you should take vinegar and goggles or a diving mask for the tear gas, so I put items like those in the car. I could not sleep the night before Friday of Rage. I was so sure that I would be arrested or killed. Early in the morning I called a friend of mine and told him that I would be taking my wife and kids to her parents' house. Initially I went to Thawra Mosque in Heliopolis. The imam there gave us a sedative shot— not a sermon but all kinds of pacifying talk about how so long as you are healthy and safe, what more do you want, and as long as you have enough to eat and drink you have nothing to complain about, things like that. It was really frustrating. We decided to go to Mustafa Mahmoud Mosque in Mohandiseen hoping there would be more people there. On the way, as we were crossing the Sixth of October Bridge, we passed over al-Nour Mosque and there must have been thousands of people there. It looked beautiful.

I took part throughout the 18 days of demonstrations. My son came with me on that first day and choked on the tear gas. In later days my wife would also join me in Tahrir Square, and I was so pleased that she came and understood. Amid the tens of thousands of people protesting every day I met people from all over Egypt.

That Friday, I saw something I will never forget. There was a man called Yasser. His face looked like he had chicken pox. He had red spots all over his face and neck. He had received a direct shot to the face with these pellet guns they were using against us, the so-called rubber bullets. His whole face and neck and chest were covered in red spots. Yet he had the most amazing spirit, some people went over to him to try and help him remove these pellets, and he refused. He said, "Go to the front lines, I am fine; go to the front and help people there break through and get to Tahrir." In Tahrir Square, on the 28th, once we had fought our way in, the people were extraordinary. I saw people bleeding but still throwing stones. I, too, was certain that I would die that day. As I was running, I felt a sudden sharp pain in my shoulder; I had been hit by a rubber bullet. I ignored the pain and looked in the direction where the shot came from and I guess it was from on top of the American University. So I ran like crazy, and a guy running beside me also got shot. It must have been a live bullet because he immediately fell to the ground and stopped moving. May he rest in peace.

During this period, I felt how strong our people are, how strong the Egyptians are. We had stopped the police, we had stopped the army. Numbers defeat power. We were gaining control and they were losing it. When the army tanks first appeared in the square, I ran up and pulled one of the soldiers off and told him the tanks could not go in. Things were very fraught initially. Some protesters smashed the headlights of the tanks, while others grappled with the soldiers. One officer told me they were not here to resupply the police with weapons, so when the first tank went in and the police did not resume their attack, we allowed the rest of the tanks into the square.

Late on Friday, I was near the museum. The army started distributing meal boxes to demonstrators in the square out of the back of a large truck. Up until that moment I had not been sure whose side they were on. By that time, the police were nowhere to be seen and things had calmed down significantly. My wife understood what I was doing, and that was a great relief for me. She prepared a bag with vinegar-soaked cloths to combat the tear gas, and a comfortable tracksuit. She even joined me for the million-man march on the following Tuesday. Mubarak's first speech divided the protesters. The day after, the square was half empty. There were those who felt he had done enough while others sympathized with the demonstrations but did not participate, and I kept trying to encourage them to come to Tahrir. I was there daily until 2am or so.

On the Wednesday, February the 2nd, there were Mubarak supporters in the square telling protesters to go home, arguing that Mubarak had made concessions. A large group of demonstrators from our side pushed them out. That day, something very touching happened. Of course, that was the day when the camels and horses attacked us in the square. They were coming closer and closer to the square and an army officer called Maged was on top of the tank that was closest to them. He blew his whistle to get the attention of his commanding officer but the officer did not respond. He whistled again and again. He was clearly gripped by very strong emotions. He was clenching his teeth and was agitated. I gave him my flag and told him that my flag had Egyptian blood on it, the blood of people who had been injured or shot by the police. He looked at the flag, then grabbed it and kissed it, and his eyes filled with tears. Another officer was yelling at him, telling him to get a grip, that he was a soldier and that he had to control his emotions in front of the crowds. But it was as if he couldn't hear him. Maged stood up on top of the tank and all the time these camels and horses were getting closer. He loaded his machine gun and fired into the air, and then when he had emptied it, he reloaded it and emptied it again into the air. We were all screaming, "The army and the people are one!" When he had emptied his second magazine, he completely lost control of himself and we actually got a doctor to try and calm him down and there is a picture all over Facebook of a doctor massaging the temples of a soldier. This was Maged. He behaved as a true Egyptian; he didn't even wait for orders.

I found a young lady sitting on the sidewalk looking very depressed. She was muttering to herself, "Why? Why are they doing this?" She was talking about the thugs. I told her that they didn't understand that we were doing this for them. She said, "I go to a British university, I have my own car, I live in a nice area, I am doing this for the less fortunate Egyptians, not for myself." So I told her that I was myself a business person and that I owned Mo'men fast-food stores, and she could not believe it. She was very surprised and asked me why I was on the streets. I told her it was not just me, my brothers were also with me and the protests were damaging our business and we were paying workers' salaries out of our own pocket. But I had to demonstrate for my dignity and my freedom. The day they sent in the horses and camels, I met some incredible people on the square.

Even though my mother called me to tell me to come home and my wife did the same, in the end my wife came to the square to show her support. I saw at that time an old man, maybe 70 years old, sitting on the sidewalk reading from the Quran. I saw a young lady in tight jeans and a sleeveless t-shirt, not at all conservatively dressed or religious-looking, holding her hands up to the sky in prayer whispering, "Allah, help us please..." with such sincerity, straight from her heart.

There was a lady sitting next to me on the sidewalk from a very poor area in Cairo called Bashteel. She had a plastic bag, I think with all her belongings in it. She said she had locked up her apartment and left her children with a friend and she had come to Tahrir to participate. She said: "I am not leaving until he leaves. Either I live with dignity or I die here and my children live in dignity." She was not talking about rising food prices; she just wanted her dignity back. I met a really poor-looking guy, who was a government employee, and he said the same thing, he said he lived reasonably well, things were not fantastic but he was getting by okay. He was in Tahrir to fight for his dignity and his freedom; it was as if he was quoting the old lady. Everybody was saying the same thing.

Then, of course, the camels and horses came into the square, there were guys with whips and some had swords and sticks and they started charging the square. That day, the Muslim Brotherhood saved the revolution. The night before the president had made his woeful speech—more anaesthesia than a speech, really—trying to get some sympathy. And indeed it had worked; half the people left Tahrir out of pity or believing him for whatever reason. I did not believe him and so I stayed. That Wednesday, the revolution could have been killed, if the Muslim Brotherhood had not defended Tahrir against the so-called Mubarak supporters.

The most difficult time of that night was between 3am and 4.30am, when the snipers started firing at us. I cannot imagine how bad someone must be in order to kill off people at random, people he does not know and who have never harmed him. A sniper must be the lowest form of human being. To be able to sit far away and just pick people off without having anything against them or knowing them or anything. For a full hour, people were dropping after being shot by snipers. This was over by sunrise prayers.

The next day, Thursday, was also a tough day. That night I went home and got some blankets, some first aid plus food and water. I was heading back to Tahrir when our car was stopped by a police blockade. The officer asked me where I was going so I told him that I was taking some food and water to Tahrir. He checked the trunk and found the things. He was very suspicious. He asked who exactly I was taking the food and blankets to. So I said I had heard there were people in Tahrir in need of help, so I was just taking these things to help. He asked me where I had heard this; I told him it was all over the television. So he asked me to wait for a while. I called my brother and told him where I was and what was happening so if I got arrested, he would at least have a lead to follow. The officer then came back and told me to go with him and he took me to Nasr City Police Station and handed me over to a military police officer.

As soon as we got there the policeman, making fun of me, told the military officer that I had been taking food and blankets to the army in Tahrir Square. So the military officer asked me if I was seriously doing that. I said I was taking them to whoever needed them in Tahrir. So then the military officer asked to check the car, and he checked it and everything was fine because there was nothing in it except food and water and some blankets. He was very polite and decent throughout, not at all like the policeman.

Then another policeman came out of an office and started asking me what I did for a living. I explained what I did and who I was and, as it turned out, he knew some people I work with and so the conversation was quite amicable. He told me that the president had done all the demonstrators asked for and we should go back home and stop demonstrating and that the Muslim Brotherhood was fuelling this. I told him I was not with the Brotherhood and I gave him someone's name from State Security who could confirm this.

Then they asked me to go with them to Military Intelligence offices. An officer drove my car, and I sat in the back with my wife, who had joined me. They had blindfolded us. When we got there, they took us into an office and sat us down. Just then, a relative of mine who worked in military intelligence called me; perhaps my brother had tipped him off. Anyway, he talked to the officer and explained to him that I was a relative of his. They walked me into an office, guiding me because I was still blindfolded and sat me down. They told me that to my right was officer so-and-so. I asked my wife if she was all right, as she was also blindfolded, and she said she was fine. They told me that my driver was also in the room. I asked him if he was all right and he said he was. Then they asked me again where I had come from and where I had been headed, and didn't I know there was a curfew. So I told them I was coming from my house and going to Tahrir and that I had heard that the curfew was not really strictly applied. Then he asked me, wasn't it enough what the president had already agreed to the protesters' demands and shouldn't we all just go home? He asked me what I did for a living so I explained again that I am a businessman and he recognized my company name and asked me what my problems were and why I was participating in the revolution, given all the president had offered. So I told him that I had sympathized greatly with the president after his speech but then, on Wednesday, events had made me disbelieve anything he said. He insisted that the president was not the one who ordered the events of Wednesday. Then he told me to lift the blindfold.

He took me to see a roomful of foreigners. He said they had all been arrested over the past few days and were suspected of espionage. I told him Egypt was now a fertile place for this kind of activity and if foreign or enemy governments didn't take advantage they would be stupid. Then I told him he had an obligation to find out who was responsible for the murders in Tahrir and to bring the criminals to justice. They finally released us without any trouble in the end, partly because my relative called again and talked to the officer holding us.

Returning to Tahrir on the Friday was like coming home. I just can't describe it. I had missed it, even just being away for a few hours. The next week was relatively quiet, not very eventful until Thursday night when there was a strong rumor in the square that Mubarak would leave that day. On the first day I had told my wife it would, with God's help, only last 45 days. Tunisia had taken 28 days to oust its president, but Egypt was a bit more complex, so I set the time at 45 days. I had no clue the system was so fragile, but then corruption eats away inside the system. There was a lot of

energy in the square on that Thursday. Mubarak was due to make another speech, and the army said we would hear good news. I sat with a friend and we both had radios glued to our ears to hear the speech. But once again, Mubarak was defiant and refused to go. My friend actually fainted with shock. Then the chant in the square rose "Yom el-Gomaa el-Asr, N'hedd Aleh el-Qasr!" (Friday afternoon, We Will Destroy the Palace With Him In It!).
—*Islam Mo'men*

"We are the ones who will protect our country."

STATE MEDIA CHANNELS LIKE YOURS HAVE COMPLETELY LOST ALL CREDIBILITY

Amr Bassiouny

Amr Bassiouny, 25, is a research manager at a leading real estate investment and development company in Cairo. He completed his bachelor's degree in Hong Kong, where his father was the Egyptian Consul. Mr. Bassiouny previously worked for Egypt's housing minister, before becoming disillusioned about the state of the country and his inability to help effect change. He surprised himself in January when he realized how passionately he felt about his country. While spending time on the streets protecting his neighborhood and protesting, he realized quickly how important it was that the revolutionaries were heard in the media, specifically on television. Mr. Bassiouny was a regular commentator and critic of the political leadership during the 18 days of the revolution. Here he describes three of these days in some depth, explains what led to his television appearances and how he and other protesters risked their lives and ransacked the offices of the secret police.

~

To live a contented life in Egypt under Mubarak, you needed money or power, and preferably both. If you had neither, every government employee (including the police) ensured your life was a living hell every time you needed to get anything done.

We also always lived in fear of the government and its secret police. They knew everything about everybody. For every 40

Egyptians, there was one police informant. These informants were doormen, security guards, shop owners or even your neighbors, and saw their position as a second income. Everybody had a file, and you never knew when it would come out and bite you in the ass. (I read many of these files when I went into the State Security Investigations Headquarters, which I will talk about in more detail later.)

I never realized that there was still a flame of passion that was left burning within me when it came to Egypt; I thought it had died completely. After the night of January 25th I found that the flame had become a wildfire that would consume my life for months, and push me towards dangers that I would have never imagined coming close to for any cause.

I took part in the protests and street clashes against Central Security Forces (CSF) on January 25th and 28th—as well as on many occasions later on against the CSF, State Security, military and hired thugs long after Mubarak had been removed. I can write of blood and bullets, or stones and Molotov cocktails, but I will choose to write my story here from a slightly different angle, how I was able to raise my voice much louder than I ever did chanting in Tahrir Square.

After the events of January 28th, I spent much time thinking of how we could continue this fight and eventually win it. Although we had followers on Facebook and Twitter, if leadership did not rise from within our own ranks sooner or later, we would lose this fight because we would not be able to organize ourselves. Seeing how tightly Mubarak was holding on to power, there needed to be somebody to unite our voices and concentrate our strength where it counted.

As the days passed, my understanding of the situation grew. I will take you through these days as they unfolded, including some of the mistakes I made along the way. This is not a complete account of all the events that happened during that time, but rather a few selected events that I will focus on.

The days after January 28th were possibly the most confusing days of my life, in fact of every Egyptian's life, as nobody had any idea what was happening and how or when it would end.

I spent the first three days after January 28th mostly guarding my neighborhood, as we were under constant attack by plain-clothed police and hired thugs, so I never got much sleep. Having played an active role in organising our neighborhood watches and street checkpoints to protect the area from thugs, as well as having had serious martial-arts training, I felt I would be an important asset to the neighborhood and therefore wasn't able to put as much time as I would have wanted to supporting the fight in Tahrir Square. I was mainly running errands, preparing myself for the uncertainty that was coming. I had to buy extra food, water and gas supplies for my family, fix my car, get my throwing knives and samurai sword sharpened and, for extra safety in the neighborhood, attempt to purchase guns from underground arms dealers.

During those three days I thought about what needed to be done. We needed to organize ourselves. While some protested, someone else needed to play politics. Without the Internet we were not able to communicate, and until we could communicate our only choice was the street. But engaging the media, specifically television, would mean we could get our message out there.

I went back to Tahrir Square on February 1st, the day dubbed as the *milioneyya*, the Arabic term for a million-man march. After having spent several hours in the square, I decided to head back home and get some food before it got late. While walking back I ran into a camera crew and chatted with them. I found out that they were working with Amr Adeeb, who is a late-night talk show host. They asked me to join them on the show that night and bring any of my friends who could speak well. They wanted us to share our views and opinions on the revolution. I gladly accepted, seeing it as an opportunity to further our cause and to get some organization back into our movement. It would be the first time since this revolution began that revolutionaries were interviewed on television.

I called my friend, Mostafa el-Faramawy, a film producer. We had spent many hours together not only talking about the revolution but also fighting side by side in the streets on the 25th and 28th. He agreed to come.

It was a dangerous drive to the studio, which was in a suburb called Sixth of October City. The show started around 10pm and ended at 1am. Being anywhere in the street during that time was extremely dangerous unless you were in your own neighborhood under the protection of its population's weapons. The production crew set up a car and driver with a special press permit to drive during curfew. We travelled in a small minibus from Maadi district and it was a frightening ride. It involved the Autostrade and up onto the dreaded Ring Road, where there was no security and where some of the released prisoners were known to stop drivers and commit violence. I didn't feel safe. At one point along the Ring Road we could see a burning tire, with concrete blocks and five armed men. They tried to wave us down, but our driver put his foot down and we screeched through a narrow gap past the blocks.

During the rest of the drive, Mostafa and I wrote down our thoughts. We agreed we needed to continue our fight, but also urge extra organization and for the Internet to be opened again and for concessions from the political leadership.

When we arrived at the studio, we were put in a waiting room with some of the other guests on the show, including three girls who would be joining Mostafa and me as revolutionaries from Tahrir. We all stood nervously before our first television appearance on the most popular talk show in Egypt when everybody in the country would be glued to their television sets.

Somehow, the moment I walked into the studio and the camera started rolling, my nervousness just disappeared. The importance of what we needed to get across to the viewer was far too serious for me to worry about anything else.

The first half of the interview was us explaining how the whole thing started, and what brought it to this extreme point. We said we wouldn't budge until our demands were met. "So, what are your demands?" Amr Adeeb asked us. I explained, "We need to first understand the base cause of this situation, how it started. This revolution started based on political demands, not economic ones. We never chanted for the reduction of the price of bread or meat, but we chanted that we wanted to overthrow the system, and this needs to happen." I then went along to explain what I meant by the system, and carefully chose my words as I knew that if I became too aggressive, I would probably spend the next few nights being tortured in a dark prison cell.

One of the memories I have from that show was when the host asked us: "So, what do you call this? All these protests and the movement you people started, what is it? A series of demonstrations?" I confidently replied: "A revolution." From then on Amr Adeeb referred to it as a revolution and the rest of the media followed soon after.

Halfway through the show Amr Adeeb put his finger on his earphone and interrupted our conversation to announce that president Hosni Mubarak would be on the air any moment, making his first statement since the revolution began. Having had complete silence from our political leadership for the past five days, this was an exciting development. Our camera went off and the channel switched to the live feed of Mubarak. We expected nothing, but to everybody's surprise he actually gave in to some of our demands. We knew it wasn't everything and we knew it wasn't going to solve every problem, but at least he wasn't going to run again for president and nor would his son. We'd made him bow down, even if just a little, and at the time that felt like a whole lot.

We then went back on the show, happy with the compromise, and all but one of us agreed the country needed some normality and that we needed to start looking towards having more stability and security, to somehow calm the situation. Looking back, I regret having said that; we were just being scammed by Mubarak and the only way to get him out was by continuing the fight.

We then had some extra discussions, where I stressed the government needed to get the Internet back online as soon as possible, in order to allow us to organize ourselves and create some sense of leadership. (This happened the next morning.) I said it would solve many problems, including reducing pressure on Tahrir and allowing us to organize and negotiate.

After the show, many people called me with praise for my approach. But my father, who is the Egyptian ambassador in Serbia, disagreed completely. He said I had been brainwashed and we were being naïve. It was just a plan to get us to calm the situation, he said. I disagreed, as did everyone else.

But he was right. The following day, thugs were sent to Tahrir on the infamous Day of the Camel when hundreds of men on camels and horses came into the square and violently attacked protesters. That's when we realized that it wasn't over. I learned the hard way. That night I went to visit a nearby neighborhood checkpoint we had set up in Tahrir Street, a 20-minute walk from Tahrir Square, and the main entry point leading from the west side of Cairo. I was horrified to find busload after busload of armed thugs driving past our checkpoints heading towards Tahrir. Our neighborhood men were too intimidated to stop them.

I was furious as I thought of my friends who were in Tahrir Square. I stood on Tahrir Street with my sharpened samurai sword in one hand and a 500,000-volt stun baton tied to my belt. I barricaded the road, tightened security on every checkpoint that I had any influence on and gave strict orders to everybody not to let a single bus or unsearched car through, no matter what. I walked for hours to several military checkpoints to beg those soldiers to support us. I eventually got two armed soldiers to block the road with us. The street patrols that night were stressful and exhausting. I went home in the early hours with blistered feet but couldn't sleep. So I set up a Facebook group, Egyptian Revolution Follow-up and Representation (ERFR), to create a legitimate voice for our revolution and planned to voice the group's demands through media channels. The group did not succeed as much as I had hoped, but we grew to 1,000 members in one week.

The Media Snowball

The week or two after our appearance on Amr Adeeb's show, Mostafa Faramawy and I had become celebrities and could not walk in the street without having people come up to us for a picture, autograph or political discussion. Within days we were getting calls from various news agencies, being offered spots on television and radio shows, as well as getting on the cover of a popular magazine—which I was too busy to see or buy. I never thought I would gain that kind of fame in my lifetime. I did not enjoy the extra attention, and being an anti-Mubarak spokesperson I never felt safe from State Security investigations and feared being arrested at any moment. I was careful when speaking on the phone not to say where I would be sleeping that night. I kept my whereabouts as secret as possible.

On February 4th, Mostafa and I were invited to a round-table discussion with several journalists at *Al-Ahram*, a state-run newspaper and media organisation. The meeting was awkward as the journalists were deeply pro-Mubarak even though they claimed otherwise. We discussed the revolution, its demands and solutions, and our comments were later published in the newspaper. I was very aggressive, saying that Mubarak needed to go and I referred to him as a thief and a murderer. The journalists did not like me very much but I think they respected me for saying it. On our way out we were constantly stopped by other journalists who recognized us from Amr Adeeb's show.

For the next couple of days, Mostafa and I started thinking about how we could use our media spotlight. During that time a group was set up that called itself the Wise Men's Council (it sounds much better in Arabic!), which included several prominent Egyptian businessmen, scientists and former politicians. They were perceived to be on the side of the revolution. Their self-proclaimed role was to negotiate our demands with Mubarak and co., though I was never fully convinced that would work. I knew they wouldn't be accepted by the people and that they would eventually fail. We needed something that came straight from the people, something with legitimacy.

I then went out through the ERFR Facebook group, which had become very active, and laid out a draft statement that we would release to the press. There was general agreement on what should be included in it. It read as follows:

> *We are members of January 25th. Our movement will express its demands in a civilized, peaceful manner. We believe in the necessity of protecting this homeland and its resources, and in response to the cooperative steps taken by the political leadership, we call upon the Wise Men's Council to represent the following demands on our behalf:*
>
> *1. Taking swift and real action to implement all promises and orders issued by the president and his*

prime minister that were made since the 25th of January

2. Implementing Clause 139 of the Constitution which allows the president to hand over all his powers to the vice-president, while allowing for constitutional amendments that may give us more space for real democracy and political freedom

3. Holding all those involved in acts of violence against the protesters since January the 25th accountable for their actions, and to publicly announce their names as soon as possible

4. Issuing a formal, written decision/order that will prohibit any arrests and to not harm protesters or political groups or any persons involved in the movement, and all those who have not been proven to be part of any criminal acts

5. Allocating a location for a headquarters for the movement until we are able to listen to the voices within our movement and to follow up our demands with the authorities, and to guarantee the safety of the headquarters and all its members

6. Issuing an official statement for the remembrance of all the brave men and women who were killed by bullets from members of the Interior Ministry's police force.

We strive for the stability of our country and pledge to protect its stability and not harm Egypt's future.

Youth of January 25th

That night we sent the document to Amr Adeeb's show, and Amr read it out on the air. Mostafa and I sat glued to the television. "This is crazy," I thought. "We just publicly ordered Mubarak to step down, on Egypt's most popular television show! Let's hope we don't get arrested for this."

Saying something like this on air pre-revolution would have been a guaranteed way to land you in prison. Just a public insult to Mubarak could lead to very serious consequences, especially with the feared State Security Investigations (SSI), and calling for him to step down was worse than any insult we could throw at him. On February the 7th, Mostafa and I were scheduled for our second late-night television talk show on Nile TV, a state-run station. We knew this one would be different from Amr Adeeb's show, and that they would be against us, but we decided to go ahead. After another unsafe nighttime drive through Cairo to Maspiro [near downtown], we arrived at the station. Many of those who worked there urged us to speak our minds and not to be afraid of being arrested. Despite the risk of what I had said on the last show, I did exactly that.

This was my favorite television appearance. When we got on air we were asked to introduce ourselves and we did so politely and calmly. Immediately after the host pronounced, "And now we have a phone call coming in from a leading figure of the National Democratic Party." I cannot recall his name or title. The caller started spewing propaganda about how he respected us and our demands and that we needed to leave Tahrir and start talking rather than protesting.

We were then asked what it was that we demanded. I quickly jumped to respond, "Our demands are clear: the overthrow of the system," which lead to panic from the two hosts. They interrupted me, saying that this would destroy the country and that our demands were illogical. I said our demands were simple and should not be negotiable. They interrupted me again with platitudes: "These things take time," "You can't have everything happen in one day" and "It's just not possible."

I started getting angry at this point and shot back, "Does it take time to sign a piece of paper to end emergency law?" I became increasingly agitated and kept shouting this question with the hosts interrupting me. In the end, Mostafa interceded and calmed the situation. He spoke for a while and while the hosts responded, he grabbed my notebook and scribbled, "Chill out!!!" I took his advice in order to avoid looking like an angry demonstrator and losing my credibility on the air.

I waited for the hosts to get into a less touchy part of the discussion and answered an easy question very diplomatically and politely. But then out of the blue I said, "...Oh and I'd just like to mention that state media channels like yours have completely lost all credibility, and you look like complete idiots in front of everybody. What was that joke you had going on during the revolution, where you had a still camera pointed at a bridge saying everything was calm—while on both ends of that same bridge people were being killed and I had to watch people bleeding to death?" This was a common joke after the revolution: that the channel had 24-hour coverage of an empty bridge on January the 28th. Before the hosts could stop me, Mostafa jumped in with another big joke: "And what about the 28th and 29th, when we were being killed in the streets, and you came out talking all day about unrest in Lebanon and said that images of Tahrir were protests in Beirut?" Seconds later, the host interrupted our joyride saying, "And this will be the end of our show today. We would like to thank our guests for joining us and a good night to you all."

That was beautiful. I left feeling like I made up for my past mistakes. I also felt a lot more worried right afterwards, afraid I would be arrested, and spent the next few days sleeping in different houses.

Penetrating the State Security Headquarters

On February the 4th, a sunny weekend morning, I drove out to the desert with a friend, near the Fayoum Oasis, to take a break from all the craziness I had been part of during the past weeks. We intended on spending the night out by a spring oasis far away from any civilization or chaos. As I was driving I was able to find mobile reception so I stopped to check Twitter, just in case anything was happening. I started reading about how the State Security Investigations building in Alexandria was surrounded by protesters, and that workers were burning their documents inside and shooting at the protesters. The second I read that, it was clear to me I would have to cut my weekend getaway short. I had a feeling this was the start of something much bigger. I returned to Cairo that night.

The next morning, on February the 5th, I heard news on Twitter of documents being burnt at the SSI headquarters in Sixth of October City, a suburb of Cairo that is a five-minute drive from my house. The second I read this I quickly got dressed and headed out there.

The Sixth of October SSI headquarters is a high-walled fortress along a highway, surrounded by desert. I arrived at 1.30pm. There was smoke rising from inside the compound, and the smell of charred paper in the air. Around 100 protesters stood outside the main gates chanting to be let in and calling for the people inside to stop burning evidence. There were also a few who were walking around the walls trying to make sure nobody was going to escape from inside. The military had two armored vehicles and quite a few soldiers blocking the entrance, keeping us at bay.

I stood around for a short time chanting with the crowd, then became a little restless and decided to roam around to see what was happening around the compound walls and look for potential entry points. I had a digital camera with me. I walked east along one of the walls and when I reached the end of it I saw a large pile of burnt documents. There were a few other people looking at them, too. We pulled some out of the pile. Most were destroyed but the few that were in good shape were very interesting to read. Most had "Highly Confidential" or "Extremely Confidential" on the top-left corner. Most of those were surveillance reports on Islamists while others were lists of names and phone numbers of informants they were using. The juiciest one we were able to pull out from that pile was a document saying that Ahmed Ezz—a prominent businessman and head of the National Democratic Party—had created a human rights group, which he would use to funnel money to Gamal Mubarak's upcoming presidential campaign to supersede his father. The document said the SSI was OK with it. That document ended up on the news the next day and created a big fuss. We loved it.

After taking pictures of scores of confidential documents, I walked back to the protest area and heard two gunshots. Everybody took cover and we realized there were snipers on the rooftops in the SSI compound. We all walked close to the

Shredded documents strewn in the corridors of
State Security Investigations headquarters
Photo: Amr Bassiouny

walls, out of sight. When I reached the south wall I found a large room inside the compound that a few other people had also just discovered. It looked like an oversized electricity room with no equipment, small windows high up near the ceiling, as well as a ditch-like opening in the ground along the length of it. Some people were able to get inside that opening, and described to us what looked like a secret underground detention center.

The army was under pressure to deal with the snipers, so they ended up sending a few soldiers inside to clear the roofs, which we cheered; still, they hadn't gone inside yet nor had they arrested the SS officers burning documents, and this made us very angry. They explained that they were waiting for reinforcements before they did so, and that they were there to protect us from the SSI rather than to save the evidence that was being destroyed.

I then heard there were low-level SSI officers escaping over the south wall so I ran over there as fast as I could. I found about 20 protesters standing in one group while SSI officers jumped the wall. Realizing that some of the SSI officers might get lost in the crowd, I raised my voice with an authoritative manner as I approached and ordered the officers to form a line along the wall and for nobody to move. The officers were definitely good at one thing; following orders. Then another group of SSI officers began jumping over another part of the south wall, so I ran there and repeated that same procedure with the help of other protesters. The military police arrived and packed the SSI officers into trucks, but we later found out they were released soon after.

An hour or two passed. The district attorney arrived and entered the compound with a few military people and the crowd calmed down a little. There was an opening in the wall and inside several of us were able to get up on a flimsy ladder and look into a room with a huge pile of burnt papers. I could see several protesters inside being ordered out by military police. As I made my way back down, a high-ranking military officer saw me and shouted at me. I went back down and looked for another way in.

At a construction site along the wall, I found a ladder leading up to a watchtower. I climbed it and then walked along the wall to the next watchtower. The district attorney and a few high-ranking military officers were inspecting the burnt piles of paper.

I climbed down near them and saw a door nearby leading to the building's staircase, so I went in and took the stairs down. Halfway down the flight of stairs I found myself standing in front of an open door made of steel bars, leading to a hallway with prison cells on both sides. I realized I had just walked into the underground dungeon of the SSI compound. For a moment I was filled with three feelings: fear, discomfort at the eerie atmosphere, and uncertainty about whether or not anybody would be inside. The desk at the entrance was unmanned and the dungeon gate was unlocked. I walked on and saw empty detention cells with their doors open. I peeked into each one before going inside, afraid I might be ambushed.

When I reached the end of the hallway I found another steel door that lead into a dark hallway. It was too dark to see the end of it. I let fear get the best of me and felt that it was crazy enough that I was where I was. I didn't want to continue any further. I walked back after taking several pictures and went up the stairs to see what was on the ground floor of the building. I found a short hallway leading to an open outdoor area, and there were about five doors to the left and right. They were all closed apart from the first one, which was a kitchen. I carefully opened a door on my left to find a room full of books, scattered in piles all over the floor and stacked up against the walls. They were obviously banned books, mostly Islamic in nature, though I didn't have the luxury of time to browse through them.

As I was about to leave, I heard voices of men coming down the hallway; they were coming my way and the door was completely open! I had to think quickly. If they were SSI officers then they would most probably shoot me, and if they were military I could be arrested. I needed to hide but there was nowhere to go other than behind the door. I closed the door and it gave a loud creak. The two men in the hallway ran towards the noise. One of them grabbed the handle and pushed the door open, taking a small step inside the room. With my hand still on the other side of the handle, I hid behind the door. I could see the hair on his head as he checked the room. He then slammed the door shut, as I stood behind it, sweating. That was a close call. I was alone in an extremely hostile place and I did not have a gun, unlike the enemy.

They had gone. I gathered my courage and explored the other rooms. They turned out to be high-level officers' rooms. One of the offices had a television set that was still on, and the other rooms had bags that were fully packed and even fresh sandwiches. It looked like they left in a hurry. I searched drawers and closets but found nothing useful. I then continued walking past the open area and into the next set of hallways, which were full of large garbage bags stuffed with shredded paper. Piles of shredded paper also littered the ground. The room that held the shredder was almost overflowing with shredded paper. Most of the doors were locked so I went up to the next floor. The first floor was the same: long hallways filled with shredded paper and locked doors.

I then went up to the second floor where it looked as if an office had been emptied out violently into the long hall. I took a picture of the mess and saw two military police officers at the end of the hallway, walking my way. I tried walking back down the stairs but they saw me and started running my way, ordering me to stop. I then walked towards them in submission, hands raised, camera in the air. I walked slowly and said I had no weapons and that I was just taking pictures. They asked who I was and why I was there. I said I was just a citizen and that I was there to expose what was happening using my camera. Then the officers saw the mess that was at the start of the hallway and asked if I was the one who had done it, saying that they would arrest me. I appealed to the senior officer and explained I was the only person who was able to get in and that somebody had to expose this sham. I asked him to please allow me to go and that I would not come back again. He told me to scram and not be anywhere near this area, as he would get in trouble if I was found by any of the other officers higher in command. I took off and laughed my way down the stairs, on an adrenaline high. That was my second lucky escape of the day.

I decided to go back down to where I had started and as I made my way down I found three other men who had sneaked in through the same staircase as I had. They mentioned that one of the offices had a computer. We entered that room and started looking for ways to remove the hard drive to take it away, which we did using a knife from the kitchen. One of the men was a computer engineer so we agreed he would take the hard drive. We exchanged numbers and then I left them. I looked back as I walked away and found two high-ranking military officers heading their way, so I warned my allies but kept walking. I went outside to find the main pile of burnt documents. It was huge and the protesters were all over it, retrieving undamaged bits of documents and packing them in empty cement bags from the construction site. I proceeded to do the same and packed a cement bag full of documents. I only had a short time to do this so I just took the 'strictly confidential' documents. I will not get into the details of these files but will only say that their contents were so sensitive to many dangerous parties that there was no way I could be safe having them in my possession. For the few days I had them with me at home. I slept with a loaded firearm next to my bed, and with an alarm at the door. I then handed the documents over to the district attorney's office to avoid getting into trouble. I felt relieved after I got rid of them in the most legal way possible.

To continue my story, I then left the compound. It was dark. My mother phoned me and as I was talking to her, I saw protesters trying to grab a tall, well-built man who was walking towards a military vehicle. He easily pushed away people as they tried to stop him. He was an SSI officer attempting to escape in plainclothes. I grabbed him in a headlock and pulled him to the ground. But he pulled a gun out and suddenly I was staring down a muzzle. I released him and moved out of the way of the gun. Tens of protesters jumped on him and proceeded to punch and kick him. Then the military violently pushed us off him and buzzed their electric batons in the air, quickly pulling him inside a tank to save him from the angry mob. If he hadn't taken his gun out, the people would not have reacted that way. We were acting in self-defense, as we all truly believed he was going to shoot me or any one of us who got in his way.

I went home that night feeling like I had experienced one of the most amazing days of my life.

"Mubarak, you are still living in the Camel Age."
Photo: Azza Tawfik

HOW COULD THE GOVERNMENT
TERRORIZE ITS PEOPLE?

Fatma Ghaly

Fatma Ghaly, 30, is the managing director of her family's jewelry business in Cairo, which was started by her mother, Azza Fahmy. With a strong inclination towards art, she gained a bachelor's degree in oil painting and began her career in the family firm's marketing department. Ms. Ghaly went virtually every day to Tahrir Square during the 18 days before Hosni Mubarak stepped down. Like many other young people in Egypt, Ms. Ghaly, who describes herself as a patriot, had known no other ruler than Mubarak. When the protests came and Mubarak finally stepped down, she describes the wealth of emotions that overwhelmed her as predominantly excitement about change, but also fear, desperation, depression and elation.

~

Everyone's a politician these days, since Mubarak stepped down. There are big discussions about what to do with Mubarak, his sons and others. These people have ruined the country, so I think it is important that the judiciary deal with them. If you have ruined a country for so long then you should pay for it somehow. At the same time, and in the bigger scheme of things, I think it is important for us not to get too dragged into the past but to move on. Putting too many resources into dealing with the past will hinder our moving forward. But unfortunately the whole country is focused on the past.

I would describe myself as a patriotic person. I have always felt that this country has a lot of potential and that we are not achieving it. I am a democrat, too, absolutely. I am Muslim by birth but I believe that religion should be something that is between you and God and should not be preached, nor enforced on anyone.

Now that Mubarak has gone, we have the raw material that can make us one of the greatest nations in the world because of our strategic location, resources, tourism industry and our young population. Unfortunately our economy, society and culture were really misused. But when I walk anywhere now, all I see is potential.

I think it started with Tunisia. The question right after the president stepped down in Tunisia was, will this ever come to Egypt? Everyone was talking about it. In many articles, analysts said it wouldn't because the people are uneducated. Tunisia is much more educated and all that. I think deep down inside I wished it would. I knew that within a year something would happen. I just didn't know that it would happen so quickly.

Mubarak's government was catastrophic. You cannot rule for 30 years and be good. You just can't, in my view. You end up becoming so isolated from the public and so self-centered that you don't do your country any good. You end up being surrounded by people who do harm because they just say what you want to hear. It's all about what's good for you and for your benefit rather than giving back to your country. It was really a bad time.

Watching events unfold in Tunisia gave me such excitement. There was no sense of fear. If anything, after the revolution started in Egypt, it just gave me more hope. If these protesters were a cross-section of the Egyptian people, then I trusted these people blindly.

We had always been threatened. Fear was embedded in us. We were taught to fear the uneducated populace and the fundamental Islamists—there was always someone to be scared of. Yet suddenly I was standing in Tahrir Square and there were all these people from different backgrounds and no one was judging anyone. Their ultimate goal was their love of their country. There was a man who carried a sign, which for me was one of the best: "I used to be scared but now I'm Egyptian."

I went there from the first day, the 25th. I went most days except for February the 2nd, the Day of the Camel. It was a day full of violence and a lot of people advised against being there. On the first day I was still at home with my friend, Hazem. We were waiting to see what would happen. All we could get on the television news was Lebanon. There had been riots there. But on Twitter it was a different reality. Things were moving, people were trying to get to Tahrir. We started feeling a bit disconnected. In the end we just went out and walked to Tahrir.

The riot police were still in action. We were in a neighborhood called Zamalek, which is a 15-minute walk to Tahrir. We arrived there at eight in the evening. It wasn't full, but I guess there were still at least 20,000 people. It was really messy. There was a lot of water because the authorities had used the water cannons and tear gas. I met a film director who had thrown one of the tear-gas canisters back at the police and had burned his hand.

People were planning to spend the night in Tahrir Square. Hazem said that if they made it through the night, if the momentum stayed, then this would be a revolution. We went home, woke up the next day and heard that the riot police had gone into the square during the early hours of the morning and lost control, shooting. Yet that morning, people started going down again. For the following two days—the Wednesday and the Thursday—there were different riots in different areas. On Wednesday the 26th, people started communicating that there would be a huge march on the Friday. But what started happening on the Wednesday and Thursday is that the authorities began cutting Twitter and Facebook. Suddenly everyone became an IT expert, working out how to hack their way onto Twitter and other networks. But the Internet was cut on Thursday night and rumors spread that they were going to cut mobile-phone lines. So on Thursday night, we were making a crazy number of calls, with everyone taking down one another's landline numbers. Text messages had stopped the night before.

Friday the 28th saw an amazing turnout at Tahrir Square. I know people who were not planning on going but were so angry about the government cutting off Internet and phone networks, that they decided to go. The government had angered many by trying to strip away yet more from them; it was unacceptable. But the 28th was a rough day; it was pretty violent.

It was the first time I had been in a demonstration. We met in Zamalek and marched onto the Sixth of October Bridge, which leads to Tahrir Square. There is a slope at the end of the bridge and the police waited for protesters to keep pouring onto the bridge, on and on. They were now right behind us. My moments of fear were mostly fear of a stampede; we were trapped in by the police. But the adrenalin was overwhelming. Even the tear gas was exciting. The only scary moment was when a riot-police car drove recklessly across the bridge, the officer inside shooting randomly. But my mind did not register it properly at the time. I saw many people get injured, but I didn't see anyone get killed. The number of protesters was unbelievable and that gave me a sense of security. And I am sure the adrenalin had quite an effect. If I had been thinking sanely at the time, I might have gone mad with fear but, actually, at the time it made sense.

We left the bridge when we realized we were not going to get through, and walked back to Zamalek. It was much safer there because of all the international embassies—the riot police were afraid to use tear gas in the area. We started the day at noon and by 5.30pm we heard on the streets that there would be a curfew at 6pm. Mobile phones were not in operation, so we just heard rumors as we walked. On the other side of Zamalek is the working class neighborhood of Imbaba, and I could hear gunshots and see tear gas. Suddenly I felt so alone. It was depressing. I asked myself whether the revolution was over: we had lost hope that people would get into Tahrir due to the amount of riot police. But we decided to walk to Tahrir Square and then head home. This was, emotionally, one of the moments I won't forget. I just felt that they had won; it was very depressing. When we got to Tahrir it was like another world. There were hundreds of thousands of people in the square: they had completely taken over. The riot police had gone, leaving their trucks to be set on fire. The National Democratic Party building was on fire.

On the 28th, unfortunately the authorities allowed thousands of prisoners out of jail. Of course, the police did not say they would be opening up the prisons but who else could have done it? There were thugs everywhere and no police. This was one of the government's tactics. At the end of the day, people want their security. The government hoped people would turn against the protesters in favor of security.

But each community began creating its own 'public committees' to restore public order. That night, everybody got organized. The youth and the men caught thugs by using super-primitive weapons such as pans and sticks. Those who had them were using guns. After this happened, the demonstrations became huge. I heard gunshots all the time. Cairo is generally a very safe city and we were not used to this level of crime. It was a scary time.

On Saturday the 29th, and also over Sunday and Monday, we were completely terrorized in our homes because there was zero security. There were all these thugs and prisoners and criminals. I think it was a tactic by the government to scare the people into thinking this was the only alternative to Mubarak's regime. I guess, after a while, when people realized it was just a tactic by the government, it made them angrier. People were asking how could the government terrorize its people, how could they make us go through this. Now there were incredible numbers of people protesting in Tahrir every day.

The square was full during those 18 days and at any point in time you had tens of thousands there. In addition to the public committees working to protect their neighborhoods, protesters also organized the security at Tahrir. In order for you to get into the square, you needed to show your ID to make sure you weren't a thug or with the government. The protest was peaceful and thugs were trying to get in and cause violence.

The day, if I'm not mistaken, the president announced that he was going to appoint a vice-president—something that he had not done in his 30 years of power. So he appointed the chief of intelligence Omar Suleiman as his vice-president. He also reshuffled the cabinet and that angered people because our specific demand was for Mubarak to dismantle the parliament—the elections of the previous November's session had been completely rigged. What he did had nothing to do with people's requests. The constitution had been changed in a way that only allowed him or his son to run for president. So we wanted parliament to change, we wanted the constitution changed. So when he came out and told everyone he was going to change the government, it was completely off.

Looking back at things, every speech that Mubarak gave at the time, every decision he made—if he'd made them only three days earlier, we would not be where we are today. It was like he was always reacting, and always too late. So people's demands became stronger, the bar was raised even higher. Not only was he not listening to what the public wanted, he also inflicted on the public all these stupid, violent, inhumane actions.

As it was, by the first week, that was it. There was no way he was staying. He had to go. The spirit in Tahrir Square was unbelievable. People helped each other. Everyone was different, but no one feared this difference. Everyone dealt with each other as an Egyptian and with respect. The whole thing was such an emotional roller coaster. I always felt that when you were in doubt, or down, just head to Tahrir. You became re-energized with the support of the people all around you and were convinced again that this was the best thing for us.

But the lack of security made many people unsure. It was fear of the unknown and it made people have doubts about the revolution. Then came Tuesday, February the 1st, when we had another million-man march. That night, Mubarak came out and spoke. For many people it was a very emotional speech. He spoke of how he had served in the war and how he would like to take six months to hand over power. That night we couldn't get any sleep. Mubarak had managed to divide the protesters. There were those who said, "That's it, enough, we got what we wanted." Others said, "That's not true, he's a liar." I believe that was the only slick move that Mubarak pulled off during the revolution. He divided public opinion.

The next day, Wednesday, the energy had changed completely on the street. I went for breakfast at the Mahani café in Zemalek and there was graffiti on the wall outside criticizing Mubarak.

Suddenly a woman burst into the café shouting: "What's wrong with you people? He's like your father!" His speech had divided us. At around noon, when I walked out of the café, I saw people who looked threatening. These were the thugs paid by the ruling party to threaten protesters that day. Standing in Tahrir Square, just the day before, I had been surrounded by close to a million people. But there was zero sexual harassment, zero verbal harassment— there was so much respect, because people were focused on one goal. But these people were different. They were rude, and they deliberately walked in my way. They looked like thugs. We didn't understand what was happening. And on Twitter, people were saying that certain government ministries were using employees at government-owned companies, moving busloads of them to come protest for Mubarak and attack the protesters. Emotionally, it was the worst day of the revolution for me.

This was the Day of the Camel. There were snipers on the buildings around Tahrir. I could not make any sense of anything. I didn't know what we should do. Back at home, I switched on the television and it was like going back in time 300 years. It was beyond anyone's comprehension that the government was actually attacking its own people. That day I had a nervous breakdown; I cried hysterically. The regime had no limits; they would stop at nothing. That was what scared me so much that day. It was a horrible day, I think the worst one. But the one good thing that came out of that day was that all those who had wanted to give Mubarak "a chance" changed their minds within hours. They saw how Mubarak was willing to pay people to attack, maim or kill protesters. The divide that was palpable the day before disappeared.

Thursday was still very intense. Two or three clinics had been set up in Tahrir. My cousin and her husband are both doctors and had volunteered to treat the injured. But there were thugs hanging around the entrances. You had to be in big groups. It was very challenging to get into the square and it was dangerous. Some people were attacked; some people were taken in by the police. Thursday was the day they really clamped down on everyone, including the foreign media. A cousin of mine worked as a freelance reporter for various international channels. He had to run from Ramses Hotel to Zamalek [approximately 2km] to get away. The military police were taking anyone in—including anyone with a camera or a press pass.

Friday was again a huge protest. Amid all the fear and the danger, the fantastic thing about this revolution was that people carried it out with a determined sense of humor. You would go to Tahrir and there would be artists' spaces where people hung artworks and banners. They used the hundreds of stones that had been thrown at them to create sculptures in the square. It was fantastic. There were concerts, there were stand-up comedians. It was a way of going through a very hard time, trying to get through it with a smile. The situation could have turned ugly at any point, people didn't care. I think for the first time in their lives, they began to feel that this country was theirs. They no longer felt they were guests in their own country.

When there was no violence, the days were just tremendous. There was a man near me who looked very poor. He had a bag of dates and offered me some, saying I looked hungry. He probably had no money to get food for the following day but he recognized my exhaustion. It was a tremendous sense of solidarity.

Then on Tuesday the 8th, we had a huge protest, just huge. I remember going to the ninth floor of a building in Tahrir and getting goosebumps as I looked down and heard hundreds of thousands singing the national anthem. It was a one-way road; this man was leaving, it was a matter of when.

On Thursday, February the 10th, we started hearing rumors that Mubarak was going to step down. Everyone got super excited that our requests were finally about to be met. The head of parliament said protesters would be happy that day: even a high official like him was saying things would happen at last. And the only thing that could happen was Mubarak stepping down; nothing else would make any sense. In Tahrir Square there was a big screen. We waited for his speech. It was two o'clock. Three o'clock passed and nothing. The hours went on. A military spokesman came out to say that the nation was "our highest priority" and said they would continue the top-level meeting that was underway. And I remember thinking that Mubarak has the highest position in the army and yet he was not at that meeting.

Finally Mubarak came out at midnight. He gave a 12-minute speech and he began talking about how he had served the country, and how he was saddened by events. Basically it meant nothing: it meant he was staying until November. There was no talk of him resigning. People in Tahrir completely flipped, they started booing and throwing shoes at the big screen. I went home to sleep. I don't think I had ever felt so depressed in my life.

Graffiti: "This is our nation, we will never go, we really hate you Mubarak."

THE REGIME HAD ALWAYS USED THE SPECTRE OF 'FOREIGN INTERFERENCE'

Atif Hussein

Atif Hussein, 35, is British Pakistani and works as an information-technology teacher in Cairo. The couple identified with the protesing Egyptians. Despite his wife being heavily pregnant with their first child, Mr. Hussein decided to take part in the demonstrations. But his experience during the time of general euphoria at Mubarak's downfall became a negative one. As he explains in this account, the protests brought a wave of nationalistic fervor that left Mr. Hussein and his fellow Pakistani demonstrators estranged and segregated.

~

As the saying goes, wherever I lay my head is my home, and for a few years now that home has been Egypt. I was born in Pakistan and after spending the first nine years of my life there, I moved to the UK with the rest of my family to join my father. For the next 19 years, London was my home. My wife, despite also being a Pakistani national, never lived in Pakistan. She grew up in Bahrain and Qatar and travelled to England for her university education. That was how we met. Our marriage and a career change from IT consultant to IT teacher took me to the north of England. My wife's experiences abroad inspired me to embrace the nomadic lifestyle, and we landed in Jordan for a couple of years before settling in Egypt—at least for now.

Experiences make us who we are and my experience has

always made me question who I am. While growing up in the UK, I always felt like a Pakistani who had moved to England. In Pakistan, I felt like an Englishman who visited every now and then. Since the age of nine I have been stuck with the label of the 'other' and, of course, the move to Jordan and Egypt did not help change that. But together, my wife and I have continued to try and fit into the communities where we lived, and have embraced the people and their problems along the way.

On January the 25th, 2011, the people of Egypt decided to stand up against the regime that had ruled over them for decades. Most people in Egypt and abroad viewed this as an Egyptian problem; certainly not one for a British-Pakistani school teacher to have much of a say on. With the exception of foreign journalists, political analysts and academics, most foreigners in Egypt also chose to see this as an Egyptian issue. But for my wife and I, living in Egypt was not about expat status. We have many Egyptian friends and like to experience life in Egypt while living among its people. Like most of those Egyptians, we did not anticipate the impact of the January 25th protests. Unable to speak the language, we missed much of the Internet publicity and only learnt about the event the following day.

It took me a while to figure out what the people were demanding as their demands included an end to poverty and police brutality; regime change; and the stepping down of Hosni Mubarak. Thursday night was my usual *sheesha* (water pipe) night with the boys and we weren't the only ones talking about what was going down. The café in Mokattam was packed and the television set, usually showing football matches, was tuned to Arabic news channels. Luckily for me, two of the guys I was with happened to know enough Arabic to translate. A politically apathetic country was beginning to show signs of becoming more politicized. By the end of the night, I was convinced that it was a good cause to join and my friends and I started to make preparations for the next day. Fortunately, Egypt's poor Internet service often encourages me to drag my laptop to cafés to make use of the free Wi-Fi. We got our logistical updates for the protest via Twitter and it was there we learnt mobile-phone networks and the Internet were going to be out of service indefinitely. But no amount of information could have prepared me for what was to come the next day.

Like many Egyptians, I too had security concerns. I may not have experienced decades of life under this regime, but I had heard many horror stories of what could happen to you if you ended up in the hands of the authorities in Egypt. The lyrics of a song by The Clash rang in my head: "Should I stay or should I go now? Should I stay or should I go now? If I stay there will be trouble, if I go it will be double." Staying at home meant accepting the mess the regime had created over the years. Going to the protest meant a possible arrest and indefinite detention in the hands of authorities known for their torture techniques. Going also meant risking never seeing my first child, as yet unborn, after nine years of marriage.

That night my wife and I hammered out all the possibilities. Although the protests in Cairo so far had not resulted in any fatalities to our knowledge, we had been hearing reports of violence in Suez. There was a strong chance that things could turn ugly on this "Day of Anger". You know you've married the right woman when she supports you in putting your life in harm's way. But it wasn't that she wanted to get rid of me. We both agreed that it was the right thing to do and the only reason she didn't join me was that she couldn't. She was heavily pregnant and literally wouldn't be able to run for her life. We decided I would go with my other expatriate friends.

I kissed my wife and unborn child goodbye and set off not knowing if I would return. Concerned about their wellbeing in case anything should happen while phone lines were disrupted, I dropped my wife off at her friend's house and we drew up a contingency plan for the day.

Instead of attending Friday prayer at my local mosque on Friday, January the 28th, I made my way to the other side of the Nile with a small group of friends and prayed at a mosque there. Marches proceeded up and down the country right after the prayer and I was among those who headed for Tahrir Square.

It could have been any other Friday. The streets were quiet early that morning. On any other Friday I would have appreciated the lack of traffic in Cairo and urged more people to stay at home to have a lie-in. But this time, the quiet on the streets was putting me on edge. Is anyone going to turn up? Will only a handful make it to Tahrir Square? Will our little group of mixed-race and foreign-looking Muslims stand out like a sore thumb and invite trouble with the Mukhabarat [Egyptian secret police intelligence]? Almost every mosque we passed along the way was surrounded by police vans and riot police.

We parked and headed towards the mosque. Since we were early, we stopped off at a coffee shop opposite the mosque. It was packed with young men, all with their laptops, BlackBerries and iPhones. As the time for prayer drew near, many headed out to wash. People were clearly there for the same reason. I suppose there is safety in numbers. For a brief period, I began to relax and forget that there was a pretty serious security threat to my wellbeing. Looking around, apart from some traffic police, there wasn't a large presence of security services. As we approached the mosque, the numbers of police personnel started to increase but remained unintimidating, possibly because they appeared without arms or riot gear. You almost got the sense that they were simply there to pray. The mosque was packed. As Muslims prepared to pray, Christians surrounded the mosque to protect us as they had said they would. It was an unbelievable show of unity.

Unable to understand the sermon in Arabic, I sat there briefly pondering the sad reality that many Muslim countries face: How security services and the people are often at odds with each other. Although sharing the same faith, the peoples' values and aspirations are often not shared by the regimes that rule over them. Security services are caught in the middle, following orders to enforce the tyranny in order to make a living. Moved by the acts of the Christian community in Egypt, I thought of lessons from history when Muslims and Christians lived together in harmony throughout the region. My moment of contemplation was interrupted by the movement of police who had begun to surround the mosque as the sermon came to an end. They were in full riot gear. Anxiety was kicking in. One of my friends whispered the translation into my ear. The imam leading the sermon had just urged the young men to be strong, reassuring them that they were on the right path. I sat there appreciating the power in the imam's speech. No wonder the governments control the sermons. They can do serious damage. His words motivated everyone and the momentum began to build. Uncertain about what would happen next, I stood up to pray. There was a wonderful sense of belonging. The cultural barrier is often broken during prayer, but this time it was different. This time, there was a sense of unity in a cause. We may not eat the same food or speak the same language, but we were all there praying for a better future.

As soon as the Friday prayer finished with the recitation of peace, there was a roar of chants—"Leave! Leave!"—referring to Mubarak. The single-word chant suited me just fine as I was able to join in. As we left the mosque and joined the Christians outside, I noticed that riot police had begun guiding the protesters towards the road like shepherds guiding their flock. The people followed. Looking around there was a sea of heads. It was difficult to estimate the number, but it certainly wasn't a handful. The roar of chants made me feel that we must be in the several thousands and we simply wanted to be heard. No one wanted trouble. I had never been in trouble with the law. The sight of batons and shields was unsettling to say the least. But we marched on nevertheless. To my surprise it actually started to feel as though peaceful protests had become acceptable in Egypt.

I am not sure if it was a deliberate tactic to wait for people to let their guard down and then suddenly attack, or if the security services were hoping that the protesters would just somehow turn around and go back, but as we neared Tahrir Square it was obvious that it was not going to be peaceful from now on. Tear gas filled the air. Initially it was just a noticeable odor but as I continued to inhale, it began to take over my senses. First the cough, then the itchy eyes and before I knew it I couldn't see and found it difficult to work out where I was. If it weren't for the women with bottles of vinegar, I may have just collapsed somewhere in the crowd. These women came prepared. They went around spraying vinegar on the scarves of the protesters, advising them to breathe in. It helped.

Apart from the tear gas, the sound of gunfire echoed among the chants. When your sight is hampered, it's amazing how the ears become more perceptive. At that time, I couldn't tell if it was live ammunition or rubber bullets that were being fired; I wasn't familiar with this setting and had never been fired on before. Our very peaceful protest was starting to become ugly. While gasping for air and with my head bent down from the constant coughing I noticed rubber pellets lying on the ground. But at that point it was not a great relief that the security services weren't using live ammunition. People were still getting hurt. We were in a deadlock, unable to move forward or turn back.

It took a while to understand what was going on. Eventually we realized why it was turning ugly. The riot police were preventing the protesters from marching on towards the Qasr el-Nil Bridge. They had blocked access to the bridge, as they wanted to prevent us from joining those already in Tahrir Square. Tear gas canisters even flew in from the other side of the Nile, suffocating those caught in the deadlock. As the police increased its use of force, the frustration among protesters grew. Some began to smash the pavements and use the rocks to throw at the police. Although this would have been self-defence, I refused to resort to violence. Caught in the middle, I had to accept my fate.

For the protesters it was the cause that motivated them; for the police it was orders from above. Neither side was willing to give in. The next hour and a half felt like a lifetime. We kept moving forward and then retreating, only to head forward again. I don't know what did it in the end, but eventually we started to move forward. The police who had been obstructing the march only minutes ago and fighting those in the front line suddenly stood aside allowing us to head towards the Qasr el-Nil Bridge. Unsure if this was a victory, I walked cautiously while some protesters embraced the young conscripts, congratulating them for defecting. Were they simply following orders to step aside and let us walk into a trap or had they really decided they were no longer going to fight their own people? To be honest, to this day, I can't be sure of the answer to that question.

Small victories in a battlefield can do wonders for morale. We marched forward feeling as though the protesters had finally got the upper hand in this cat-and-mouse game. We reached the long-awaited bridge and it appeared that the security forces were not going to try and prevent us from crossing it. By the time we had reached the end of the bridge, it was time for the midafternoon prayer. Protesters congregated to pray. Once again, the police chose the end of the prayer to make their move. We had just finished praying when we were showered with tear gas and rubber bullets. The sound had become a familiar one by now. Thousands of people's lives were put at risk by this cowardly act.

Those in the front line were pushed back by water cannons. Others tried to duck, seeking protection from the flying rubber bullets and tear-gas canisters. Panic kicked in and people started to run back. The tear gas was unbearable and I even contemplated jumping off the bridge at one point just to get away from the crippling effect. To avoid being stampeded, small groups of people made human chains to move. I'd lost track of my friends long ago, but fortunately found one of my students and his father and hooked up with them.

We retreated but by now there was mounting anger and the protesters became even more determined to proceed. I stayed clear of the bridge. Tear-gas canisters labelled with "Made in USA" filled the street. For a brief moment my anger was redirected at the US government. Why would the United States supply a dictatorship with tear gas? As I sat on the pavement to get my breath back, I watched the injured retreating. There was a lot of blood from where they had been shot at with tear-gas canisters at close range. I cannot begin to imagine what it must have been like on the front line. But despite the risk, there were plenty of brave and strong young men who continued to march forward, some even grabbing the canisters and hurling them back at the police.

The sun began to set in Cairo. The protesters had stood their ground and gained victory. The police retreated and that was my cue to head home. You do not really appreciate mobile phones until they no longer work. Fortunately, my friends and I had agreed to meet at a petrol station right after sunset in case we lost contact. Heading back took much longer than anticipated. Seeing cars on fire at various points on the route home was a sight I had not expected. This was not what I had signed up for and I was glad we left when we did. I did not want to be associated with any violence.

When I finally reached my wife's friend's home, I don't think she could have been happier to see me. She'd been glued to the television set, as was everyone else in this extended-family Egyptian household. I think they had been flipping through every news channel in both Arabic and English. I sat in the kitchen having a cup of tea, watching footage on Al Jazeera of the violence on the Qasr el-Nil Bridge. I could not believe that I had just been there.

Returning home, glad that the day had finally come to an end, we got into bed amid rumors the police had been relieved of their duties for the time being. The army had appeared on the streets. Tomorrow was to be another day of protest. After today's violence, the regime surely had to go.

Chaos marked the beginning of the day, on Saturday, exactly as Mubarak had threatened. My wife was woken up by a phone call. Carrefour, a major shopping center, had been looted. Again I dropped her off at her friend's home and set off to meet the boys for our second day of protesting before we went back to work on Sunday. We parked as close as we could to Tahrir Square and continued on foot. We couldn't see any uniformed police on the streets. Civilians directed cars to control the traffic. Who would guarantee security was anyone's guess.

The army presence was very noticeable. The tanks look much larger in real life than they do on television. It was quite an intimidating scene and the uncertainty resulted in an atmosphere of caution. It is one thing to confront the police, but it's quite another to mess with the army. It still wasn't clear whose side they would choose to be on. The burnt-out cars lining the streets increased the sense of unease. How was this going to end?

After being searched by the army, we entered Tahrir Square. I tried to join in the chants as much as I could, but the hundreds of thousands were doing a good enough job to be heard. Though Mubarak seemed to be oblivious to the demands of his people, they seemed to be getting louder and more resilient. I don't know if there were more people who showed up on this day, but their presence was certainly significant. We stood with the crowd but no one really knew what was happening. Everyone stood facing the Ministry of Interior so that was what we did as well. It was a bit strange joining a cause that had no leader directing it. At various stages, the organic nature of these protests created doubt

A soft-drink advertisement urges youth to "Be Happy" while a burnt-out State Security vehicle presents reality on the street

within me and I often felt uninformed. I could see snipers on the rooftops of buildings circling Tahrir Square and as the dead bodies started to come in, the realisation kicked in: yesterday's victory was only the beginning of the battle. It would have to get worse before it got better. It took a while before we learned what was happening. People were trying to make their way to the Ministry of Interior and that's where the bodies were coming from. I counted at least four. The sound of gunfire echoed in the square.

This Egyptian protest was full of symbolism. Shoes thrown at pictures of Hosni Mubarak; graffiti belittling the regime; the burning of the National Democratic Party headquarters; police vans being stormed by civilians—these were all powerful statements for anyone who had lived under this regime. But in this country, the Ministry of Interior was the mother of all symbols of oppression, and I guess that's why it had become such an important goal for the protesters. They were bent on marching towards it even if their lives were at risk.

With mobile-phone networks down, communication was largely through word of mouth (and in my case, through sporadic translation). I pieced together what was happening. The protesters had a strong will to head towards the Ministry of Interior but there was no barrier between them and the Ministry to protect them from the gunshots coming from inside the building. The protesters began urging the army to move their armored vehicles forward so people could take cover behind them. These massive tanks were certainly enough for us to take cover. Ducking behind one myself, I could hear the gunshots as I crawled forward over the bullets scattered on the ground. I seriously feared for my life. All that stood between me, unarmed, and the policemen firing live bullets indiscriminately was an armored vehicle belonging to the army, whose allegiance was still uncertain.

Somewhere along the way, mobile phones began to work. I managed to ring my wife and tell her that I was okay. She told me that rumors were going around in Cairo that looters were having a field day. Prisoners had apparently escaped and were going around creating havoc. Relieved that she wasn't alone, I hung up almost feeling like I was in another country. Tahrir Square had a different air about it. In contrast to the rest of Cairo, this was where the people were in charge.

Fear kept creeping in. The friends I was with gave me great strength and the rational discussions in my head helped re-energise the courageous part of me. Then I saw a woman in a full veil [niqab] sitting on top of an armored vehicle, chanting with passion and waving her hands in the air. I remember thinking, if she can do it, what am I afraid of? I looked around and saw teenagers, kids and even old people marching on.

As it began to get dark, the protesters started to leave the square. Word had got round that prisoners were on the loose in the city and most men felt they needed to head back to protect their homes. By the time we had grabbed a bite to eat and headed home, groups of men had already organized themselves as vigilantes, policing the streets with makeshift weapons, stopping and searching vehicles. On our way back I was informed that schools would be closed for the next few days. That suited me as I don't know how I would have managed a day at work.

My wife and I decided it wasn't safe for us to be alone in our flat for the night. She decided to stay at her friends and I made my way back with my friends to guard their home. Reaching home was a mission in itself. Almost every street had a civilian-manned checkpoint. I had just returned from a mini-war zone with armored vehicles and live ammunition flying around, and here I was being stopped and searched by kids whose heads hardly made it above my waist. Why had Mubarak's government taken the police off the streets? How had prisoners managed to escape? Why was it that other key buildings remained protected, such as embassies and ministries, but not the prisons? Questions bounced around in my head all night.

We set up a fire outside my friend's residence and took shifts. The entire street was lined with groups of men trying to do their best to keep their homes safe in the absence of police. The same was true at my wife's end. As I struggled to stay awake everyone discussed politics, speculating about what was to come.

On Sunday morning, news channels were reporting that up to 6,000 prisoners in a prison in Fayyum had escaped and that organized looting was taking place all around Cairo. What kind of a regime sets prisoners loose on its own people just to stay in power? This is a city of rumors. Maybe after decades of controlled news people here have become accustomed to "spreading the word" to pass information. By the morning, almost every household had heard the same story—that gangs of thugs were going around looting the city and the streets were no longer safe as the police had disappeared. There was a sense of chaos with everyone panic-buying. We, too, set off to stock up with some basics. It was easy to understand why shops were running out of goods. If you found a shop that had eggs, you rang everyone you knew and stocked up for the clan. Supplies ran out within minutes. I was guilty of this, too.

In a sense, I think the chaos achieved its objective. Many people that day became distracted with immediate domestic issues, so that protesting for the future of a nation was temporarily put on hold. Security and supplies became the topic of discussion and the uncertainty inevitably led to some people feeling less willing to protest. Discussions that previously demonstrated excitement about the future of Egypt now seemed to focus on a fear of the unknown. Mubarak had already stated that he would not run for another term. More people seemed to be willing to accept this compromise now than before. The chaos was becoming too unsettling for them. But notably, these people were not among those who had lost their loved ones in the protests. The briefly united Egypt was starting to divide again.

Amid the uncertainty, my wife and I decided to stay at home for the next two days. We needed to figure out what the objectives of the protests were going to be before we decided to support them. Much of our time was spent in front of the television, flicking through Al Jazeera, the BBC and CNN and comparing their version of events and how they chose to portray them.

Tuesday was supposed to be the million-man march. My discussions with various groups of people had made me wonder if the numbers would show. Out of principle, I couldn't sit this one out. My friends and I set off for round three of protesting, hoping that this would be the straw that broke Mubarak's back.

Entering Tahrir Square was far more difficult this time. The army had blockaded much of the area, tightening the entrance and exit from the square. Still unclear of the army's intentions, I wondered if we would be able to get out in time should things get ugly on the inside. But once again, the sight of women and children helped me put things into context. Fear spreads like a disease and courage like a cure. For decades this dictatorship, like many others across the Arab and Muslim world, had ruled with fear as its main weapon. It was becoming clear that fear was going to be the tactic this regime would continue to try and use to quell these protests. Giving in now would be a waste of the blood already spilt. Worse still, giving in now would mean an even uglier future. With these thoughts, I passed through the army security check and faced the friendlier search points manned by civilians.

By the time we got inside, the square was already packed. The atmosphere was more what you would expect at a carnival rather than a protest. We filmed people to capture the moment. Egyptians have a knack for chants and for the first time, I could appreciate the Egyptian sense of humor. I sat around soaking it all in, filming and photographing those sights I thought were my Top Ten. But admittedly, the best ones had been captured by the media.

Here are my Top Three, translated, though I'm sure they sounded better in Arabic:

3. A man holding a cat with a sign saying: "Leave! Even the animals don't want you."

2. A lady carrying a baby just few weeks old, with a sign saying: "Leave, grandpa!"

1. A man holding a placard stating: "Leave, my wife needs to give birth and the kid doesn't want to see your face."

Within a few hours, the square was packed and it was practically impossible to move about. It was a sea of people. I had spoken to my wife a few times and she said that the aerial shots on television were amazing. There were definitely more than a million people here. Military helicopters circled the area, but people remained undeterred.

I am not claustrophobic, but for the first time in my life I was able for feel for those who are. To get some air, we decided to walk to the other side of the square. Half an hour later we finally reached the other side and couldn't have been more pleased to see a Tahrir Koshary shop on one of the side streets [koshary is a traditional dish made with rice, pasta and lentils]. Not because I wanted to eat, but because aside from the protests taking place, I was probably witnessing a rare moment in Egyptian history: people formed a queue stretching almost 50 meters and no one was pushing in. Everyone seemed to be bending over backwards to be accommodating. The rich stood with the poor, united by a cause. As I watched the queue bend around a corner while people waited patiently for some food on this hot day, the name 'Tahrir Koshary' couldn't have been more appropriate. The branch in Nasr City could have pots piled with an endless supply of the stuff and yet someone will still jump a queue of three people. But not here in Tahrir Square. It was like, *I'll wait my turn and if I don't get any, then bon appétit to the guy who took the last of it.* That was the attitude and I loved it.

The remainder of the day passed in soaking up the atmosphere and music. At sunset we began to make our way home. The day had passed without violence. Was this really going to become the Hyde Park of Egypt? Would people be allowed to protest but be ignored by a government that would continue to do what it wanted anyway? We had reached our numbers but when would we achieve our goal? Would Mubarak stay and just let people protest? These questions marked the end of the day. Concerns about the effects of the protests on the economy had already begun taking place in households. Outside of Tahrir Square, Egyptians seemed divided on how hard to press for their demands. The next big day was being planned for Friday.

On Wednesday morning, I helped a friend run some errands and we deliberated about going down to Tahrir Square. My wife called me and advised me not to go as word was going around that the army was arresting foreigners. After yesterday's peaceful experience, I did not think there was much of a threat. But the army's ambiguity as to whose side they were on was sufficient reason to exercise caution. Small protests by groups of people calling themselves "pro-stability" had begun to appear in cities around Cairo. The people were becoming increasingly divided.

The wealthier classes seemed to want an end to the chaos sooner as they feared losing all they had worked for. Worries that the protests would continue to fall on deaf ears, and in the process society would come to a halt, seemed to spread and heated debates started to take place in living rooms (as people stayed home from work). State-run media remained in control of the flow of information and people seemed to lose focus of what they had set out to achieve. In the absence of leadership or a clear method to bring about change, many people seemed willing to settle for cosmetic changes packaged as significant gains.

My friend and I decided to play it safe and skip Tahrir Square. With the Internet back on, we opted to use the time to Tweet and share information online so people could know what was happening in Cairo. Unaware of the risks, a couple of my friends had already decided to make their way to Tahrir Square. All was well until the sun went down.

Images of men on camels and horseback attacking protesters began appearing on international media outlets. It could have been a scene from an old Omar Sharif film. Unable to understand Arabic, I wasn't sure what the official stance was on this incident. But I did hear claims that the authorities were innocent of these acts of violence, and that the men on horseback and camels were tour guides from Giza who were attacking protesters for hindering the flow of tourists and their livelihood. I was not sure who came up with this explanation, but it was laughable. It had been taking me hours to reach Tahrir Square due to the searches and road blockades and I had a car. How did these men make it all the way to the Nile from Giza on horseback and camels—and go unnoticed and unimpeded?

Tweets began to appear about violence breaking out at Tahrir Square. Liaising with our friends at Tahrir, we began our own little reporting mission. One friend was a doctor who immediately jumped in to help the injured; the other went around gathering video footage and sending it through BlackBerry Messenger for us to upload.

The news coming out of Tahrir Square was horrifying. Groups of men were attacking the unarmed and helpless protesters, throwing Molotov cocktails at them. As the violence continued some of the protesters captured the attackers. Their IDs proved that they were security service personnel and my friend photographed this for us to share with the outside world. The entire night was spent uploading information and Tweeting. With the odd power nap, it was mostly an all-nighter. One of my friend's mobile phones had died, so our correspondence was hindered. They sat it out until dawn and as soon as the curfew was lifted, they began making their way back home.

Hours passed and our friends didn't show up. We had expected it to take a while, but eventually it became clear that something was wrong. Initially unable to reach them on the phone we had assumed that this other phone had died, too. But I decided to try it one more time. I heard it ring and then someone picked up. The initial relief was replaced by fear. No one spoke, but there were footsteps, lots of them; the sound of heavy boots sent a chill down my spine. They had been arrested. After about 16 hours of waiting, which must have seemed like a lifetime for his pregnant wife, one of the two who had been arrested made contact. He was on his way home. The other, the doctor who was helping out at Tahrir Square, appeared a few hours later. Their experience was enough for me to distance myself from this revolution.

Egyptians were being fed paranoia that "foreign elements" were behind the chaos. This was always going to work against me. These two friends of mine were detained simply for being foreigners. On their way home they were stopped by the local vigilantes and handed over to the army. Once detained, they were blindfolded and beaten with no explanation given. They simply had the wrong color of passport. Disheartened by their experience, I could no longer feel part of this revolution. These friends and I had literally risked our lives to see this country work towards a better future, and we did so feeling like one with them. But the feelings suddenly didn't seem mutual.

Egyptian nationalists viewed every non-Egyptian's involvement with scepticism. The Mubarak regime had always used the spectre of "foreign interference" to muster support for its actions. It was doing it again. Foreigners were now being blamed for the unrest. My support for this revolution would be considered an outside agenda to destabilise Egypt. I felt betrayed. This was a sad ending to my role in this revolution.

I sat out the following protests and marches. It had become a movement solely for Egyptians; there was no room here for people like me.

The banner reads "Leave."

Spray-painted slogan on a disabled Central Security Forces vehicle: "Peaceful"

THEY MADE HIM THINK NOBODY IN THE COUNTRY WAS CAPABLE

Salah el-Shamy

Salah el-Shamy, 68, is owner of a medical equipment trading company. His family is from Menoufeya in the Nile basin. He is a widower and father of three, and lives with his youngest daughter. He also has two other daughters. Here he contrasts the reality of living under Mubarak's rule, with life as he knew it under Nasser and Sadat. The way Mr. el-Shamy sees it, Mubarak was never a real leader and had lived off the glories of his predecessors.

~

I have witnessed three presidents: Gamal Abdel Nasser, from the time of the revolution against the king in 1952 until he passed away; then President Anwar Sadat; and then, of course, Mubarak.

I remember during the days of Nasser, we were always asked to tighten our belts, consume less, be frugal; this was what Nasser was always asking of the people. There were a lot of things that were not available; it was not easy, but nobody complained that they couldn't afford fruit or they couldn't afford to eat this or that. And certainly there wasn't this feeling of suffering you sense around you now. Maybe because there were no extremely rich people? Or maybe because there was not much corruption? Or maybe because we felt we were being asked to tighten our belts for good reason? Because we have a national dream we must achieve, maybe? There was no suffering like we have these days in Egypt.

The majority of the people loved Nasser and they were always waiting for him to appear in a parade or a radio speech or television when that technology came into our homes. People had a great deal of respect and love for him because he created the strength of the Egyptian character. He gave us our confidence and national pride. We were proud of him, and of ourselves. Countries all over the world changed because of him, from South America, to Africa, to the Middle East and even in Asia, revolutions against occupation were inspired by his actions and words. Countries that were living in political darkness were shown the light of freedom by Nasser's Egypt. He was a symbol of our freedom, our individual and national freedom. Egypt was not just a country then, it was a leader of the free world. This was the case until Nasser was joined by a group of subordinates who were not sincere, as history has shown. But during his time, we were all proud to be part of the Egyptian era which helped free people all over the world from colonialism and suppression. We were proud to be part of that generation. I am one of many people who would have carried Nasser on their shoulders if called upon to do so. We loved him; he had given us our pride and dignity.

Sadat was the most capable politician to rule Egypt. He was exceptionally intelligent and had immense political acumen. He was also brave and took calculated risks. At one point we had large numbers of Soviet advisors and experts involved in every segment of Egyptian society, especially in the army. Every army unit had one or more Russian advisors. Egyptians felt there was no way these people would ever leave Egypt; we thought they were here to stay. And then, shortly before the 1973 war, as if it were the easiest thing in the world, Sadat simply kicked them out. He was a strong, fearless leader. At the same time, life during Sadat's days was good, we did not suffer. People made money and lived well.

The relationship between people and the police has always been bad—during Nasser, Sadat and Mubarak. The people have never liked the police force, because historically they have always had far too much authority and power, more than they needed or deserved. So much power that, at some points in our history, police officers felt they were more important than army officers. They had better benefits and were given privileges that army officers did not have, even though at the national level, the army is so much more important. These benefits were not just official. For example, if an army officer and a police officer both went to a fruit stand, the salesman would give the police officer higher quality fruit at better prices, simply because the police officer had the power to make life miserable for the owner if he did not do this. The army officer had no practical authority whatsoever.

Sadat also gave Egypt a high international profile. I travel a lot for my work and during that time people abroad would frequently ask me about Egypt and Sadat. This was especially true after the 1973 war. Nasser had wanted to retrieve the land occupied by Israel but had no resources to do so. Sadat had enough political intelligence to make full use of those same limited resources to cross the canal and get into Sinai. This was the only way the Israelis were ever going to be willing to return the land they had stolen; a show of force was the only language they could understand.

In terms of corruption, it was much more rare then than during Mubarak's time. There were a handful of corrupt businesspeople close to the regime at the time, and the scale of their corruption was relatively limited. But during Mubarak's time, things got completely out of hand—corruption was on a huge scale; it was almost organized. When you think of all the people who were in power for any period of time before the current revolution, and you look at the amount of money stolen and land given away, it was almost as though they had inherited this country and were just deciding how to split up a personal inheritance. It was never that bad under Sadat.

When Sadat died, Mubarak became president by default. He had no political weight whatsoever, he had no character and was bland and weak. As you might expect, the people around him started polishing him, defining his character to make him look good. They tried to create a leader from nothing. One positive about him [to his credit] was that he had led the main air-force sorties against Israel in the 1973 war, but so what? This was just one of many manoeuvres that won the war. Reading the papers and watching the news over the past thirty years, you would think that those sorties were the only thing the Egyptian army did during those fateful days of October, 1973. But it was just one small part of the whole attack, which was actually led by Sadat!

From the day Mubarak became president to the day he was ousted, he was living off Sadat's glory. He consistently reminded Egyptians of freeing the Sinai, but it was Sadat who had led and started that, not him. I think the biggest problem during Mubarak's time was the people who surrounded him. They deified him, they made him think nobody in the country was capable of making any decisions or doing anything for Egypt other than him. He chose these people very badly, and this led to a large group of people continuously telling him that everything he did was correct, never criticising or challenging his decisions, no matter how disastrous.

One of the worst problems that erupted during Mubarak's time was the divide between Christians and Muslims. This was never a problem ten or fifteen years ago. We did not know these problems before. Until just ten years ago, I had never thought about who was Christian and who was Muslim. I have always had Muslim and Christian friends and we were one group; there was never this division that we have seen recently. That happened during Mubarak's time. I am not saying he created the trouble but he should have been responsible for resolving it or at least making sure it did not spread, but he did nothing. He watched it grow and did nothing.

The same thing happened with the economy: he watched it collapse. He watched ministers and other officials rob the country and did nothing. He was responsible. He was President. How could he allow a handful of businesspeople to completely control the economy like this? The same happened in politics. The parliament was hand-picked by a few kingmakers who controlled all political life in the country, again under his watch and with his knowledge.

When the demonstrations started [in January], I thought it was just one more demonstration that would be dispersed by the police as usual. But as time went on, there was a persistence that we had not seen before. I started believing it may go all the way. More than two years ago, I started predicting that something would explode soon in Egypt and my first worry was the impact it would have on the country. I expected that the revolt would come from the government or from the poorest segments of society. But actually, it was regular, middle-class people who led the revolution—not the army and not the poor. Most interestingly, it was all over Egypt, and not just in Cairo, which made me really believe that it would succeed without being destructive.

SO THEY SHOULDN'T LOOK AT WOMEN—BUT IT WAS ALL RIGHT TO TORTURE PEOPLE?

Najah Nadi

Najah Nadi, 25, is a student of Islamic Studies at Al-Azhar University in Cairo, the world's oldest university and Sunni Islam's foremost seat of learning. This year, she starts her graduate studies in philosophy of religion at Boston University. Ms. Nadi was one of Egypt's young demographic who took to the streets on the first day, then told her supervisor she would be off for a few days to continue the fight.

~

January the 25th was a Tuesday, so, as usual I attended my Arabic linguistics class at al-Azhar Mosque. My plan for the day was simple: go to class, do some work, then join my friends who would already be at Tahrir Square. I had no great expectations for the protest. I had attended several protests recently, particularly those organized by the "We Are All Khalid Said" Facebook group, in reference to a young man in Alexandria who died last year in a café after being terribly beaten by policemen. The case horrified Egyptians, who were angered by the subsequent denial by the police. You got used to hearing about protest campaigns for one thing or another. Of course, while I hoped the protests would get the country to carry out reforms to assuage public anger, particularly in the wake of the uprising in Tunisia, I just assumed that this protest would be like all the others.

At 4pm, my friend and I headed to Tahrir Square to join the protest. We took a taxi and when we arrived at a nearby street, the driver said he couldn't get any closer to Tahrir because the streets were closed, and State Security police blocked all entrances to the square itself.

As soon as I walked into the square, I realized that this protest was different. The others were organized by a set group of people. They were demonstrations by lawyers, or by students or workers, for example, with specific demands such a wage rise. But this appeared to be a multi-class protest, with a far larger number of people involved. You could just tell from the clothes people wore that there was a mix of rich and poor here. As we started to interact with the other protesters, we were able to join discussions about the situation in Egypt, about what had happened in Tunisia, and whether or not it could happen here. Would the Egyptian government understand our demands and agree to the much-needed reforms for a better country? The protesters around me were talking about their experiences with the government. Sometimes it was an account about price rises, or pointless laws, or how they or a family member had suffered police brutality. People were trying to motivate and inspire each other, and they were successful. We were moving and chanting in groups. It was not very organized but it seemed to all come together. Buoyed by what was going on around me, I decided to call other friends to invite them join this unique gathering, but the mobile network had been disabled. After 7pm the numbers started to increase. A friend of mine told me the police in Ramses Street had started arresting some of our friends and were using tear gas to disperse the demonstrators. In Tahrir they had also used tear gas before my arrival.

By 8pm, we joined protesters trying to march to the National Democratic Party building. But the police prevented us from reaching it. I decided to go home and return the following day. On my way home, I called several friends to tell them about this great event and get them to come along. I was unable to sleep, my mind was full of the events of the day—of the bravery I had witnessed, perhaps some sense of my own bravery, and wondering what would happen next.

On January the 26th, I woke up with energy, determination and enthusiasm. I went to the office but told my supervisor that

I needed to take some days off for the protests. I called friends, and put up Facebook postings to urge everyone to go to Tahrir and support the protest. There were small protests that day and the next in some side streets, but everyone was preparing for the big one: Friday of Rage on January the 28th. My friends and I planned to go together. We asked activist friends to recommend a spot where a large protest would take place. They recommended the al-Istiqama Mosque in Giza, where opposition politician Mohamed ElBaradei was due to pray and join the protest. But unfortunately, the phone lines and Internet network were cut 30 minutes later, so I couldn't contact the friends I was planning to go with. The government thought that by doing this they would stop us all from going. But it had the opposite effect: it made us angrier. We wanted to keep going, to demand our rights, that we be treated respectfully.

I decided to go by myself. My family was very worried and urged me not to go because they feared the State Security police. I told them Allah would protect us protesters. I went to the mosque two hours before the Friday prayer, at noon, and found the same high spirits and the same determination among the protesters. The numbers had grown, and there were many journalists there. Even though different protesters wanted different things out of the revolution, they all shared the same dream of freedom.

When it was time to pray, people feared the police would lock the doors of the mosque, so we decided to pray outside. State Security police surrounded us, because they knew we planned to march to Tahrir Square. I was amused by the fact that a senior police officer ordered the policemen to face the other way, so as not to look at the women as they prayed. So they shouldn't look at women as they prayed—but it was all right to torture people as part of a regular working day?

After the prayers, we chanted loudly. We vastly outnumbered the police. They started to use tear gas and water cannons on us. Some of the protesters began to throw stones, but we stopped them, chanting "Peaceful! Peaceful!" It was impressive the way some of the protesters formed a protective shield in front of police cars to prevent others from destroying them. After about ten minutes the police stopped the water cannons and tear gas.

Hundreds of us were now on the move and we started to chant, "Our People, Come and Join Us!", addressing those who looked on from their buildings, and those who were in the streets. Many of them joined us. I naïvely believed that the police had given up trying to stop the protest. But I was wrong.

When we reached Cairo University's Faculty of Engineering, near Giza Zoo, we were ambushed. Tear gas was thrown at us from several directions. We had brought vinegar and onions to help against the tear gas, but it wasn't much use. The tear gas was too intense for us to even look for the vinegar we had. It was awful. People were vomiting; some fainted. Others were running, hoping to find a place to hide. The only place available was the engineering faculty buildings but the doors were closed. We asked the people inside to open the doors but they refused. Some students inside helped us break down the doors and get into the buildings. It was a very dangerous situation—people were suffocating from the tear gas, they were panic-stricken and scared. It was a large crowd. Many of us managed to get inside the faculty's garden, but then, the police started throwing tear gas bombs in there too. It was terrible to know that they did not care if they killed us. Every time I choked on a new bout of tear gas, I thought I could not stand anymore, and that I would die there.

In 20-minute intervals I would start chanting again and try to move on. But the tear gas hit me again and again. This went on for three hours and we were getting nowhere. In the end, we decided to escape through the nearest side street, which was too narrow for police cars. We ran in small groups to reach the side streets and many families there gave us water and Coca-Cola, the latter to help with the effects of tear gas on our eyes.

After such a terrifying day, I decided to go home. On my way home, I saw many fires and was told by the taxi driver that several police stations across the city had been set alight. When I got home I was so exhausted I went to bed. My sister woke me to say that Hosni Mubarak was giving a speech, his first since the protests had begun. I was optimistic. I felt that he was listening to our demands for political reform. I didn't know at the time how many people had been killed by State Security police. There was no reception for mobile networks or the Internet so it was virtually impossible to communicate with other people. In the morning, I was shocked by the scenes of destruction I saw on my way to the office. Cars had been destroyed, there were army tanks in the street, buildings were charred or still burning, I saw blood. People were talking to soldiers and giving them food. Egyptians respected the army for announcing in Tahrir Square that they would not use their guns on Egyptians.

I returned to Tahrir Square. I was so worried about my friends, but found some of them among the thousands of Egyptians who had gathered there, with the army observing. We talked about the murders perpetrated by State Security across the country and how, despite my initial optimism, Mubarak's offer to change the government was just a ruse. But we still felt it was a good start. Maybe we could keep the pressure up and demand more radical reforms. Mubarak, however, still refused to get rid of the emergency law. The jails were then opened to allow thousands of criminals to roam the streets. The lack of security was very frightening. We realized after these developments that we would have to continue protesting until the entire regime stepped down.

It was incredible how Tahrir Square became a new, free Egyptian city. It became a stage on which we could all practise freedom of speech; it was a space that brought together all aspects and levels of Egyptian society. On Tuesday, February the 1st, I met Sheikh Emad Effat in the square; I had attended his class at al-Azhar University before joining the revolution a week before. I asked him about our class at al-Azhar, and he said, "The lesson is right here. I came here to learn, and so should my students." I was so happy to hear this from my professor, and was happier when the number of Azhari sheikhs and imams increased daily, alongside the thousands of al-Azhar students who joined the revolution. Tahrir Square provided a great forum for people from different backgrounds and religions to learn more about one another. There was plenty of humor, too. The spirit of Tahrir spread across the country. Because the police had disappeared off the streets and there was no security, public committees were set up, with men and youths assigned to protect neighborhoods and search the cars of those traveling through their areas.

There was still plenty to fear. As the government became

increasingly desperate, feeling its power slip away, it varied its tactics to scare us. Thugs, mercenaries, and plainclothes police were paid by Mubarak's party to use violence in the square. Many protesters were seriously injured in attacks on the square, but at the same time it showed Mubarak's regime for what it really was. There was no pretence any more. These violent actions just strengthened our resolve to continue. We knew there was no going back. The strength of the numbers in the square, and the sense of camaraderie helped us stay calm. We shared food, blankets and tents.

Thousands of protesters in Tahrir Square felt sufficiently safe on February the 10th, because of some security measures we had implemented—like checking people as they came in through the entrances. Many felt safe enough to bring their children along. But some of us wanted to raise the pressure elsewhere. About 3,000 of us went and stood in front of the National Democratic Party headquarters, while others went to the president's palace. Mubarak was due to give another speech. We all expected him to step down. But then the disappointing announcement was made that he was just delegating his powers to his vice-president Omar Suleiman, whom everyone hated.

It was Friday, February the 11th. I decided to join the group that was protesting in front of the presidential palace in Masr al-Jadida. At the outset there were only about 3,000 protesters there, but the numbers soon swelled, with some coming from Tahrir Square, some from other cities. The military begged us to leave the palace, saying that if the republican guards heard any gunshots, say from thugs or hooligans, they would think we were attacking and would return fire, resulting in a bloody battle. We understood their fears but refused to move. We needed to be here to demand our right to freedom of speech, and to be free citizens.

I FIGURED THESE WERE A BUNCH OF KIDS WITH SOME SIGNS AND BANNERS

Maged Abdel Wadood

Maged Abdel Wadood, 45, is a business owner living in Cairo. He has a degree in economics from the American University in Cairo. He is married, with one son. Having worked for more than a decade for a number of multinational companies both in Egypt and in the Arab gulf region, he set up his own company providing security systems for clients' houses. While he recognized there were faults in the system under Hosni Mubarak—the fact that you needed contacts, the often-rough treatment by police—he also felt Mubarak was a good leader. While improvements were needed, Mr. Abdel Wadood is not a keen advocate of democracy, having watched the disintegration of Iraq following the American invasion in 2003. He felt that the Tahrir Square demonstrators wanted to change things too quickly.

~

Before the revolution, and throughout my life, I have always been critical of the way things are done, of the way we are as Egyptians. I love this country; I cannot imagine living anywhere else. I did live abroad but chose to return. I am very vocal about my criticism of Egypt, which angers many people. But over time, I have adapted and became able to cope with the way business is done here. I do not like politics because I think politicians are liars; I don't know of a single honest politician. I was never interested in politics. I remember a few years ago, someone invited me to join the National Democratic Party during its heyday, when Gamal Mubarak [Hosni Mubarak's son] had just started getting involved in actively running the party. I was invited to join one of the committees. But I figured it was a lot of talk and no action, so I refused.

Politically, I dislike a lot of how things are done, but I am running my business and I have to adapt. I spend 80 per cent of my time fire-fighting in this country. Let me give you an example: I need to price my products but I can never do so accurately. I will import a consignment of products six times a year—the same quantities each time—and I get billed for customs and import tariffs differently every time. When I pay taxes, it is always contentious. The tax authorities don't believe the figures we present and always insist that we are making more money than we claim to and they demand that we pay higher taxes. Their estimates are arbitrary and the reality is, the taxman just wants a bribe, and I hate doing that. I mean, if on a personal level I want to help the taxman out because he is a low-paid government employee, that is my right, but to have to pay a bribe just to be allowed to pay my taxes fairly, I just hate that. There are two annoying things about that. First of all, why should I be hijacked like that? And second, the taxes we pay are not really used for the improvement of public services or infrastructure. Instead of going into the country's treasury, it goes into some government official's pocket.

The government pays no attention to me as a small or medium enterprise. I go to a bank and ask for a loan of say 500,000 or a million pounds (US$80,000 - $160,000) and they say I need to have a deposit of a million pounds. Does that make sense? They should be helping small and medium-sized businesses! And it's not as if this is policy—some tycoon can walk into a bank and receive hundreds of millions of pounds in loans with no more security than his name. Shouldn't they be doing the opposite? I mean if you help businesses like mine, you are helping the whole economy grow. This is what made America great, all the small and medium businesses. We started off with five employees, today we are 40. If the government supported me instead of hindering me, we could be 300. That's 300 new jobs, 300 families with income, and the government will receive more taxes. I could have grown many times as quickly as I did if I had received support from the government. These are the kinds of things that angered me.

I was never worried about being thrown into the back of a police truck for no good reason, as happened with some people, because I had contacts and I could call someone to get me out of any situation I found myself in. But what if I called someone and they were not available, or asleep? I could be treated very badly by the police until I was able to reach someone with some influence who could help me. This abuse of the law was horrible. It was all about who you knew and what contacts you had. But at least I never felt any personal insecurity. The door of my house did not need to be locked. Why? Because we had one of the lowest crime rates in the world. This is a country where there is no rule of law, but you feel safe at all times. My wife could come home by herself at three in the morning and I would not be worried about her safety.

When the revolution started, I thought these kids with their utopian ideals had no idea how the world is run. I remember writing on Facebook: "These guys are like Alice—as in, Alice in Wonderland."

Of course democracy is great, but it is not for Egypt. Take Iraq, for example: the US invaded in 2003 and Saddam Hussein was removed in 2006. That was four or five years ago and to this day, that country is in complete chaos. Some countries are well-suited for democracy and some are not, and I fully agree with [former vice-president] Omar Suleiman when he said in an interview with Christiane Amanpour that Egypt was not ready for democracy. Everybody was in an uproar about that statement.

I liked Hosni Mubarak as a person. Considering who he is, the kind of treatment he has been given over the past 30 years, his background as an army officer, I would say he is an exceptionally humble person. I was at his house maybe two months ago for some installations. I thought: "This is where the president lives? I am not impressed." I have been in many nicer houses than his. Though the furniture was expensive, it was pretty dilapidated and not what you would expect to see in a president's house. I walked for maybe three minutes from the engineering office in charge of his residence to the house itself. Nobody stopped me, and there weren't many security checks. I was told to enter the house, and I said, "This is it?" It was a bit messy; there was an outbuilding that was clearly added later to house an elevator, and Gamal Mubarak had some kind of penthouse on the top, nothing fancy at all. I remember thinking, this was not the White House.

I don't think Mubarak is great, but he has done a lot of good for the country. For 30 years he kept us out of wars that we could not fight. We would be annihilated if we went to war, because who would we go to war with? Sudan? Libya? No, we'd go to war with Israel. We have a great army but we're no match for the Israelis. Most of our weapons come from America and sooner or later, in a war, we would need spare parts; and then we would have to turn to Uncle Sam, and we know whose side the Americans would take! Uncle Sam would just say "Uh-uh, you shouldn't be fighting." So, Mubarak kept us out of wars. He was one of the key players in our victory in 1973. And he is a nice, down-to-earth man. I spoke with him on a couple of occasions and he is a very simple, funny man. He does not come across as a politician; he seems quite ordinary. My problem, of course, was with the entourage that surrounded him. They were dirty liars, who painted a very bright picture for the president, making him believe everything was perfectly fine; that Egyptians had great lives, that they were happy and loved him. These were the people who deified him.

So I liked Mubarak, but there were things that bothered me. I did not like the fact that we had a very indecisive stance on Israel. I wanted to be more aggressive with them. But apart from that I was happy. Of course, there are poor people in Egypt, there are people who suffer. But are you telling me democracy will solve these people's problems? Sorry, go to the United States, you're walking down a main street and there's some poor man living in a cardboard box, shivering from the cold, eating out of a trash can, and they have democracy, right? People here need to understand that democracy does not mean an end to poverty.

When the recent demonstrations started, I figured these were a bunch of kids with some signs and banners, dreaming of democracy, so I didn't pay much attention. What I did not realise at the time was that this was clearly well-planned and there was lots of money behind it as well. When the Central Security forces started attacking the demonstrators I thought, "Yes, get these young people off the street. They've had their say, they've had the demonstration, they've expressed themselves. Now let's move on."

I believe in taking things one step at a time, and not rushing into everything at once. It would be great to be able to fix everything in one try, but you cannot predict what the consequences of massive, sudden change would be. So I figured, after the demonstrations, we should take this one step at a time. Maybe if I were a teenager or in my twenties, I would have wanted to demonstrate and get things done all at once. But with age, you moderate your position somewhat and are more mature. You want things done gradually.

Some of my friends call me very right wing, but I am not sure what that means. I have a point of view on some things, I am willing to listen to others and can be convinced if their argument makes sense. So I understood what these kids wanted, but now we need to get back to business. And I knew from previous demonstrations how the scenario would unfold: the youth would go out to demonstrate, they might get violent; then one shot would be fired, one youngster would die, and the whole thing would be over.

But that did not happen this time! This time was the exact opposite of what usually happens. I figured it was related to the oppression, the anger, the frustration; it was as if the youth were saying, "Enough, leave us alone, let us say what we want, listen to us and change things, we have had enough oppression."

When the demonstrations continued, I asked myself if I supported them. I have the same frustrations as the kids on the street. I know people might think I have an easy life, but they don't realise how hard people like me have to work to live the way we do, and the pressures we face. I had told my wife before all this began that we would soon have a revolution led by the hungry; a revolution led by the poorest of the poor. I actually spoke to an uncle of mine about helping me get a gun licensed but my wife did not like the idea at all. She called him and asked him not to help me. What I actually expected was the poor to revolt and attack us,

The National Democratic Party headquarters building burning, in what some observed to be a 'methodical' fashion

Unscathed sign at the burnt-out National Democratic Party headquarters: "For a safe future for your children, vote NDP."

instead of the government. Now, after all these events, my wife regrets that she stopped me getting the licensed gun, because I had to buy an unlicensed weapon. I have a responsibility towards my family, and I thought I could protect them with a gun.

The reason I was convinced it would be the lower classes that would revolt is because people like us, who typically have the brains and money to do something about the political situation in our country, have too much to lose. But it came as a surprise that kids from our social class were involved in this. If my son had been five years older, I am sure he would have been involved, too. I am not against change, I am for it. But it is not just Hosni Mubarak who must go; the whole way this country has been run since former president Abdel Nasser must change. If you remove one old general, Egypt will be run by all the other old generals of the army, and it will continue this way unless the demonstrators try to remove the army itself.

All the demonstrators have achieved so far is to help the army get rid of one of their own, so another of their own can take over. This is my point of view. The army behaves like it owns the country. If you want to see where all the money is going, check the army. US$70 billion [the reported size of Mubarak's hidden wealth] is a ridiculous estimate, and not even a monkey sitting in a tree would buy that figure. Bill Gates doesn't have that much money.

Anyway, it happened, and it was carried out by our sons, by people from all classes. I respect that; we needed change and we needed the right to be able to speak our minds. But we also need to remember the obligation we have to speak responsibly. I am not sure this was the best way to do it; I think other methods may have produced a higher level of democracy.

Personally, I had no problems with government agencies or in getting paperwork done or whatever. I could pull strings to get things done, but not everyone is in that position. People have a right to have their paperwork finished without having to pay a bribe, without having a friend on the inside. But for that to happen, government employees should be paid a decent salary and should have good reason to come to work in the morning.

It is understandable that they expect bribes when they can barely survive themselves! Another problem was that the law was applied very selectively. I could be carrying a kilo of hashish and I could get off scot-free because I am the son of this or that important person. But someone else would get arrested for a minor offence because he has nobody to protect him. The law should be applied equally to all. Also, the emergency law was abused. Under this law, a State Security official could have someone arrested if he didn't like the way they looked; there was too much abuse of power under the umbrella of emergency law. These were the major issues I had with the country. And in my view, the rest of the problems could have been dealt with at a later stage: free elections, free press, those could have been sorted later.

Let me tell you about an incident that took place when we were running neighborhood watches during the demonstrations. An old BMW drove into my area; it had darkened windows in the back. We stopped the car and asked for identification. It turned out the man driving it was a State Security officer and the passenger in the front seat an army officer. We asked them to roll down the back window, but they said that it wasn't working. So we opened the back door and found a huge man inside, with his hands between his legs. We asked him first to place his hands where we could see them, which he did, and then for his ID. This he refused, claiming he did not show his ID to just anybody on the street. We told him he would not get through unless he produced some ID. I stepped back from the car and yelled to the others manning the blockade that this car should not be allowed through.

So this man got out of the car and walked towards me. I immediately undid the safety lock on my gun. He stopped and yelled, "How dare you raise a gun in my face?" I said very calmly, "I haven't raised it yet." He seemed to stop and think for a second; then he smiled widely and said, "You are our brothers, and we are all brothers, here is my ID," and he pulled it out to show us. It turned out he was a State Security officer. We all laughed after the car left. It felt good to see them humiliated for once.

What worries me now is the lack of security. We had security in Mubarak's time. My sister lives alone with her children, my mother lives alone, and I also have to take care of my wife and son. On the first day of the protests, my brother, who lives in Dubai, called to say he would send a chartered plane to get us out of Egypt until the situation stabilized. When I heard this, I told my wife to prepare to leave for Dubai within three hours. I called my mother and sister and told them to pack. But when I told my son, he said he was not going anywhere. He was adamant. "I am not leaving," he said. Then my mother and sister called and said the same thing: "We are not going anywhere, we are not leaving our family and our country and escaping." They were very tense days. Sometimes I would come home to find my wife crying.

I wanted Mubarak to stay in power until September and then hand over. When you resign from a job in a company, it takes a few weeks or a couple of months to hand over a job. Mubarak had an entire nation to hand over. This is Egypt, one of the most complex, powerful, populated countries in the region. How could they expect him to hand it over in a day? He should have been given more time for two reasons. One, he was never a Saddam Hussein who gassed his own people; and two, he did a lot of good for the country as well. He deserved to leave with dignity, not to be kicked out like a criminal. He was a man who put his life on the line for his country; not many people have done that. I don't even know if I could do that for my country, but he did it more than once.

THINGS ARE NOT AS DANDY
AS THEY MAY SEEM

Rasha Ragheb

Rasha Ragheb, 37, is an Egyptian Christian. She currently works for the International Management and Finance Academy; she has also worked for six years in Jordan for the Higher Academy for Banking Sciences, an Arab League organization. Her interests lie in the development of people and education. While she comes from a Christian family, Ms. Ragheb fasts with her Muslim friends during the holy month of Ramadan and partakes in other festivals. She describes herself as a patriot, and was not in favor of the demonstrations at Tahrir Square. She felt they were misguided, influenced by foreigners, and that it led to a humiliating departure for Hosni Mubarak.

~

I was raised in a house where there was never a difference between Christians and Muslims. It is true that I am Christian myself, but I know very few other Christians. I pray with my Muslim friends in the mosque during Eid. I fast during Ramadan with my Muslim friends because it is just not right for me to eat and drink while they fast. My Muslim friends celebrate Easter and Christmas with me, and have even helped me decorate our Christmas tree. This is just the way we are. If I look back at my life and try to remember the happiest days of my life, they were those spent with my Muslim friends, and the same applies to my family. My views are not related to my being a Christian.

I consider myself very patriotic. I have never thought about leaving Egypt or living elsewhere, and the time I spent in Jordan was not that long. I have never spent more than 45 days outside my country. I like to travel but this is where I live; I love Egypt. I have always felt proud of being Egyptian. Since the revolution, I have heard many say that now we can be proud of being Egyptian, but I have always felt proud of being Egyptian, of holding that large green passport.

But maybe five or six years ago, I started feeling this was not the country I have always known: this was not *my* country. It was the first time in my life that I ever considered moving away. Religious extremism was on the rise. Never before had I heard, while walking down the street, someone say, "God have mercy on her", because I was not wearing a veil. I dress modestly, yet I still heard these comments. In fact, I started seeing very strange clothes all over the streets of Cairo. I understand that some men grow beards to express their devotion to Prophet Mohamed, but why wear a short galabeyah? Why wear Pakistani clothes? We are Egyptian! If you want to act or dress according to Muslim code, do it the Egyptian way.

I felt there was nothing I could do to fix things, and this too made me feel as though this was no longer my country. I disliked the fact that I could not contribute in any way. I hated that there had been a political blackout since the days of former president Gamal Abdel Nasser. I did not like that my political choices consisted only of the National Democratic Party. I could not join the Muslim Brotherhood, and I don't like them anyway. I don't like it when people address me according to my religion. It is my own business whether I pray in a mosque or a church or a synagogue, or whether I am an atheist. People should engage with each other's minds. If I am a productive person and I love my country, then that is all that anyone should be concerned with.

When the demonstrations of January the 25th happened, I felt guilty because I had been grumbling for the past five years about how education was going down the drain, and how young graduates were of very low calibre. It is not that we didn't have jobs; it is that we didn't have people who could work well. And you couldn't blame them because it was not really their fault or even the government's fault. It is a combination of problems.

Another very serious problem in our country is corruption.

I am not against people making profit, but I am against people stealing from the country and giving nothing back. Egypt is a very rich country, but it was being robbed blind. As a result of this severe corruption, millions remain in poverty. Why should a wealthy minister be able to make a deal to get a palace for peanuts while he already owns homes all over Egypt? Why should he get land worth tens of millions in the center of town and pay next to nothing for it? Why this immense greed and corruption? I got desperate to the point of saying to myself: "If they want Gamal Mubarak to be president, then let him be president, but let this corruption end."

People think we have been dead for 30 years since Mubarak took over. But the truth is that we have been dead since former president Gamal Abdel Nasser's reign. And what really scared me was that people in Tahrir Square were carrying posters with Nasser's photo! So, I was very much against what was happening in Tahrir. I knew something would happen as a result of all the corruption, and people would explode, but I was against it when it happened. Not against the idea, but against the way things were being done; the execution was not right as far as I was concerned.

When people first started going to Tahrir Square, I figured it was exactly the same as previous demonstrations, which had been carried out by various opposition groups including the 6th of April movement and Kefaya (Enough) groups. Of course, I am a firm believer in the right to demonstrate, but I was also convinced that it was futile, that the government would treat these demonstrations in the same way it deals with everything we did, with complete disregard. The attitude has always been, "Let them talk, let them do what they want, but in the end we will do what we want with this country. Let them have their fun, they cannot affect us."

But then, day by day, the numbers started increasing on the streets, and I thought, "Maybe this time it's different." For the first few days, when things were picking up momentum on the streets and the president did not respond at all, I thought maybe he had died. We actually had a bet going on at home, about whether he had died or not. What if the president had come out on the first day, the very first day, and promised that he would step down at the end of his term and that his son Gamal would not be made president? I am sure everybody would have left the square right there and then. Anybody who had a hidden agenda would have had no excuse to stay on in the square. I still cannot judge whether it was good or bad fortune that Mubarak did not do this and that the events escalated this far. What are the circumstances that led to all of this? I am not yet able to call it a revolution because I am not aware of all the dimensions of the events. It was clear that many parties were doing a lot of suspicious things, and I am still unsure what exactly happened in Tahrir Square and who did it. One of the many fears I had was a result of the first act of treason that occurred on the Day of the Camel. If Mohamed, Jesus and Moses came down from heaven supported by a troop of angels to swear to me that Hosni Mubarak had ordered this attack on the square, I would not believe them. Not because Mubarak is a good man, but because he is not that stupid. I think the groups that planned and executed the attack were people who would have benefited from the continuation of Mubarak's regime. Whether they were National Democratic Party members or members of parliament, they were benefiting from the regime and did not want it to collapse. This was how they were used to behaving when dealing with a problem—beat up the kids and they would leave. But I am certain it wasn't the government itself.

My second fear came about because all the State Security offices and prisons across Egypt were attacked at once using the same technique, but no other government offices were affected. My father, brother and uncle are all officers or ex-officers so I know the police very well. Good or bad, they would not empty out their stations like this. This was a coordinated attack with external planning. This made me fear that some foreign influence was coming into the equation.

Another fear gripped me. When I actually started going to Tahrir Square, I did not like the way it looked. I found members of the Muslim Brotherhood everywhere. I found some newspaper reporters, a few television personalities and some young people, but they were not the dominant force in the square; it was the Muslim Brotherhood.

Someone I know, a young man whose income was badly

affected by the events, decided to go to the square himself and talk to the young people there to try and get them to leave so he could get back to work. He told me that the Muslim Brotherhood stopped him and almost hit him, and they beat up another man who was also arguing for people to leave the square. Another person I know saw a foreign lady who was giving children five Egyptian pounds each to spray-paint "Leave, Mubarak!" everywhere. So certainly, there were external forces at play here, with hidden agendas. State Security had already informed the Minister of Interior that large numbers of people from the Far East, from Lebanon and Palestine, had rented houses near Tahrir Square over recent weeks. I am not a conspiracy theorist at all, but I believe all of this was caused by something beyond what we could see.

Also, this idea that Muslims and Christians were praying together in the Square is just nonsense. I don't mean that we hate each other; only that things are not as dandy as they may seem. Muslims and Christians united only as a reaction to the catastrophe of the complete disappearance of the police—which I believe was orchestrated by Habib el-Adly, the former minister of interior, who thought it would make people beg for the police to come back.

My ideal scenario was that after the first speech in which Mubarak promised more political freedoms and an end to the state of emergency, people should have gone home—not to give him a chance, but to give us a chance. We have been failing in politics for half a century. Would we suddenly be able to run such a complex country? We needed this chance to learn politics and learn how to run a country. I heard once about one of Prophet Mohamed's companions, who was asked whether he preferred a strong but non-pious man or a weak but pious man to command an army. His response was that he would rather have a strong man who was not pious commanding an army. And his explanation was that a non-pious man's lack of piety harms him but his strength will be directed to commanding the army properly, while the weaker man's piety may get him into heaven, but his weakness will reflect poorly on the way he commands the army. And so I did not like the idea of all these passionate people, without any experience, taking over the country. We needed time until September to hand over the country to a new leader.

I am also scared of people who are unwilling to listen to different opinions. People are only interested in talking, but not in listening to others. "Everyone is corrupt, everyone should be thrown into jail!" This cannot be the right way forward. The youngsters who participated in the demonstrations do not listen to anybody. They are in the driver's seat now and that is why I am scared! We need to listen, and not just talk.

On top of all of this, I am scared of the Muslim Brotherhood. At the beginning, they said they would not go into the streets. But when things started growing more serious, they said, "The youth of the Brotherhood want to participate and we will let them." After it was all over, they claimed credit for the protests, saying the Brotherhood did all of this for Egypt. And then there was all this talk about martyrs. Who were these martyrs? If some man carrying a rocket-propelled grenade launcher attacks a police station and the police officers inside fire back and kill him, does that make him a martyr?

This is the situation we are in, regardless of what I like or don't like, and now we are in a position of having to choose. We are in the middle of chaos and the only organized entities we have are the army and the Muslim Brotherhood. I think we would all choose the army because it represents stability and it is a known entity. We all want to get back to work, send our kids to school, get on with our lives. I feel sorry for children in this country; what kind of future do they have? Our economy is a disaster; we probably need 15-20 years just for our economy to get back to where it was before January the 25th.

Does the Facebook generation understand this? Do they understand that we need the best person for the economy to be president? If Gamal Mubarak is the best person for our economy, then we should have him as president. It does not matter if he is a nice man or not. The country needs someone who can get the economy back on track. We do not want Pope Shenouda III [head of the Coptic Church in Egypt] and Sheikh Ali Gumaa [Egypt's Mufti and a top Islamic scholar] ruling the country. I am not looking for the nicest or the most pious people.

MOST EGYPTIANS ARE RELAXED, LAID BACK, PASSIVE, AND SEE NO HOPE FOR SERIOUS IMPROVEMENT

Amr Abdullah

Amr Abdullah is a businessman and former Chief Strategy Officer for Vodafone in Egypt. Here, Mr. Abdullah tells about the attitudes of his well-to-do neighbors who were largely against change or sceptical about it, and about the German au pair who arrived with some determination in the midst of the revolution.

~

I live in Gardenia, a gated community of well-to-do residents. Villa prices are in the US$1-1.5 million range. Some of the residents are close friends of Gamal and Alaa Mubarak, the former president's sons. The general demographic of the place consists of well-educated professionals or business owners. The reaction to the events in Tahrir Square within this community was very interesting. The majority were completely against the revolution, simply because their status quo was not so bad and certainly better than what might follow. They were driven by fear of what might come. They were all worried that the Muslim Brotherhood might be behind this whole thing, or that a bunch of hoodlums were causing all this. They pictured the country disintegrating into chaos, and never seeing their money again. Some made plans to leave the country forever if things did not return to normal soon. This was the general atmosphere.

They all started buying weapons; the number of guns that were bought during that period was incredible. My neighbors in Gardenia thought I was crazy because I wasn't considering leaving. I had no gun and no intention of buying one. We formed a public committee like everyone else in Egypt to stand guard at the compound gates at night. But I did not stay at the gates for long. I felt most of these sessions transformed from guard duty to hang-out sessions. People just chatted and had fun. I did go a few times but only if there was something concrete to be done. For example, if the guards got cold, we lit a fire to keep them warm. But apart from that I was not interested in being there just for the sake of feeling I had done something useful. There were a lot of uncomfortable discussions, especially with the friends of Mubarak's sons. When anyone spoke badly about them or about the president, they would take these comments personally, which I could not understand. These people were public figures. When you talk about a public figure, you must accept that people will have different opinions.

What the residents did during this time was primarily to secure themselves. They blocked the gates completely, put up barricades; someone brought two machine guns in order to feel prepared. But nothing happened at all.

When I told them I was planning to go to Tahrir with my family, I began to feel real pressure from them. They all told me I was insane to go, especially with my family, because it could get violent. But I was very happy when I went. The first day I went to Tahrir was the Tuesday before the famous Day of the Camel. I remember writing on Facebook that it was more like a carnival than a revolution. Most of the people there were middle and upper class, though of course, all levels of society were represented. This was true until the Muslim Brotherhood's presence became more apparent, because the Brotherhood represents all social levels. I have to say, if the Muslim Brotherhood had not been in the square on the Day of the Camel, this revolution would have failed, because they were the ones who protected the square from those attackers.

I met four people I know in the square, people who have businesses or who are investors. The total worth of these four people easily tops 10 billion Egyptian pounds. One of them was severely beaten the following day. What this showed me was that these four people were, in spite of their wealth, willing to go to the square and take personal, physical risks, unlike the people in my compound who were nowhere near that wealthy. When I went back home, I felt I had a responsibility to create some awareness among my neighbors. Most people in the compound had no clue what was going on in Tahrir. They did not even consider going there an option. I started recording on my Facebook wall all the important things that were happening in Tahrir, to create awareness. I think I regularly reached 700 or 800 people. I started inviting people to join me in Tahrir and everyone refused for some reason or other. Some because they were friends of officials in the previous government, others were worried about their personal safety, and yet others were afraid their businesses would be affected negatively by the revolution.

But the truth is that the scene in Tahrir was fantastic. There were no issues there at all, not between religious and non-religious people, Muslims and Christians—everybody got along. There was an unbelievable level of acceptance, which is really the normal thinking of ordinary Egyptians. Whenever I went home my neighbors were curious to find out what was happening in Tahrir. They thought I was insane but heroic and brave to have gone there, but when I showed them pictures and videos I had shot in the square, they were finally convinced that it was not as unsafe as they had believed. Gradually, some said that they would like to go see for themselves. More and more felt confident that it was the right thing to do. One of them felt very patriotic, another knew some of the people I had met in Tahrir and was encouraged by that. One of the people I met in Tahrir was the boss of a neighbor, who then decided to go, because if his boss was there, he should be there, or else it would reflect badly on him at work. One man took food to Tahrir and distributed it among the demonstrators. The attitude was changing, but not overall.

Maybe 20-30 per cent of my neighbors started going regularly to Tahrir. The rest refused to go. These were the people referenced by the saying, "The sphinx would conduct a revolution before the Egyptians do." Most Egyptians are relaxed, laid back, passive, and see no hope for serious improvement in the country. All they hope for is to get another citizenship, other than Egyptian. Their main concern during the demonstrations was where they could buy food, how they would feed their own people. They are not bad people, but they are a group of people who just want to get by.

There is an interesting observation here: the billionaires I saw in Tahrir were not afraid. These guys who are not worth more than one or two million dollars were more worried about their million bucks than the billionaire was for his billions. This might be why the billionaire is what he is; he has the vision to see beyond the immediate risk and into the future. He is willing to take the risk to get what he wants.

I would like to tell you about the German au pair who came to live with us, right in the middle of the revolution. She was supposed to arrive on January the 30th but a few days before that, I gave her a call to tell her it was probably best that she postpone her flight for a few days. I did not want to frighten her off completely because then she might just have refused the job; but at the same time, I did not want her to come during all these events, because if it were one of my children who was headed for a similar situation, I would not want them to go. I told her it was best she wait a few days until things settled.

But she insisted that she was not afraid. I could not convince her to postpone her flight, especially because she said she had contacted Egypt Air in Germany and they had assured her that flights would be running as per schedule. As it happened, she went to the airport and they delayed her for eight hours. Then she called an hour later and said the flight had been cancelled so she would be coming three days later. Three became four, but on the fourth day she did indeed arrive. The very next day she was in Tahrir with my wife and children, waving an Egyptian flag alongside Egyptian demonstrators.

THE NDP BUILDING WAS STILL ON FIRE. HOW COME WE COULDN'T SEE ANY FIRE ENGINES?

Mona & Ziyad Rushdy

Mona Rushdy is the wife of Hatem Rushdy, this book's editor. She was born in the United States to an Egyptian father and German mother, and came to Egypt at the age of 10. She went to a German school before later graduating with a bachelor's degree in Mass Communication and Psychology. As well as being a full-time mother of three, Mrs. Rushdy is a student of the interpretation of the Quran, working towards certification to become a teacher of the Muslim holy book. The Egyptian revolution gave her, she says, her first real sense of Egyptian patriotism.

Ziyad Rushdy is a 15-year-old student. He is the son of this book's editor. Previously uninitiated in politics, he participated daily with his father in Tahrir Square.

~

Tuesday, January 25th, was the day I had planned to go away for a couple of to my parents' summer house on the outskirts of Alexandria. With my husband at work and the kids at school, it was going to be just my mother and myself. When I heard there was to be a demonstration in Cairo, I decided to go on with our plan because my mother had been looking forward to getting away and I did not want to disappoint her. The weather was perfect, the drive was smooth, we took our time—we were happy. We arrived at Carrefour shopping center, where we had lunch, walked around and watched a movie. We were in touch with our family members in Cairo, who told us that demonstrations were under way there and had also started in Alexandria. By the time we left Carrefour, things were getting violent in both cities. There were rumors that the entrances to Cairo from Alexandria were closed because they wanted to prevent demonstrators from reaching the capital.

We decided to head back the next day. Thousands of people from Alexandria were heading towards Cairo by train, as well. When we returned to the capital, we were relieved to find the entrance to the city was not blocked but we got stuck in really bad traffic jams. The demonstrations were by now in several parts of the city. It took us double the usual time to get home. My mom spent the night at my place because it seemed it might be too dangerous for her to go home. She left early the next morning.

Thursday, January 27th: mass demonstrations were planned for Friday and I had to participate. I wanted to start by making banners to use and to distribute to the protesters. My husband told me he would finance the project but that I had to keep the cost as low as possible. It was the end of the month and money was scarce; the banks had closed and we didn't know when they would reopen. I cut up some boxes and used the sides to write on, and bought some extra cardboard from the stationery shop. I had paintbrushes at home and I bought black and bright red paint. I decided each banner should have two sides: the front in Arabic and the English translation on the other side for the foreign press— the world had to understand what we were demanding. First and foremost, we wanted free democratic elections in September with no possibility of an inherited presidency. We wanted: "No More Repression!", to "End the Emergency Law!" and to "Free All Political Prisoners!" It was one o'clock in the morning when I finished and the 20 banners were perfect!

Earlier that day I had discussed going to the Friday demonstrations with my husband, Hatem, but he didn't like the idea. He figured it would be too dangerous because, as everybody knew, the police could react viciously. I also wear the niqab (the full veil) and my husband felt this could make me more of a target. But I was determined to go, just like so many other people. Finally, my husband said he and my 15-year-old son, Ziyad, would go and check out the situation. If it felt safe enough, they would come back for me.

Friday of Rage, January 28th: I rose early and started soaking small pieces of cloth in vinegar, packing them into small plastic bags, taping them shut and sticking labels with the instructions "hold against nose in case of tear gas" onto them. I made about 30; two for my husband and son—I saved one for myself in case I could go—and the rest to be given away. Ziyad and I chose vests with lots of pockets and we stuffed them with the anti-tear gas remedies.

I left the house with my husband and children at around 8.30am because, very inconveniently, my youngest had a table-tennis tournament starting at 10am, about three hours before the demonstrations were due to start. We went in two cars. The banners were too big to fit into the trunk of my car so my son and I put them on the back seat and covered them with a sheet; the big bundle in the back looked quite suspicious. My husband dropped our two daughters off at the sports club and met us near the Mustafa Mahmoud Mosque, one of the main meeting points for the demonstrators. We then went to look for a place to hide the banners until after Friday prayer. We drove around the mosque area a few times but couldn't find one. Some of the men hanging around that area looked like they might be secret police, so we decided we needed to get out of there before we attracted any attention. I parked the car at the end of the street and left the banners inside. My son and I got into my husband's car and we drove back to the club.

On the way, my son noticed he no longer had mobile coverage—strange. Actually, not strange, because earlier at home we had no Internet access either. Mubarak at work! Soon my husband and I, and everybody else, had no phone coverage. Was Mubarak that scared? I was starting to get uncomfortable about Hatem and Ziyad going to the demonstrations—this did not feel good. But I knew they had to do what they had to do.

So when and where would we meet? How would I know if they were okay? How would I know if I could join them? We decided the meeting point would be every hour, on the hour, in front of the table tennis hall until 6pm. If they didn't show up, I would go with the girls to my parents-in-law's house, which is just a few minutes away. We would wait there till 8 or 9pm and then go home and hope for the best.

My husband and son watched the first of my daughter's two matches before going to Friday prayer. (She won that one.) Then it was time for them to go to the designated mosque, so we exchanged car keys because my husband had to try to get the banners out of my car right after prayer. I have never appreciated mobile phones more than at that moment. I would not know how things were going and anything could happen—they could get hurt, disappear, even die.

My mother-in-law had joined us in the meantime. We also met one of my youngest daughter's favorite teachers from school. She had left her two small children with her mother at home; I didn't ask where her husband was. Of course, the hot topic was what was going on in the country right now. The teacher was yearning to go to the demonstrations, just as I was. It's at times like these that you wish you were single and had no responsibilities.

My daughter had her second game—she lost. She didn't play as well as she normally does—she must have had her father and brother in the back of her mind.

It was prayer time now, so we all went together to the mosque in the club. The imam's speech was emotional. We prayed for the demonstrators and I could not stop my tears flowing. I was so worried. But I pulled myself together; I had to be stronger than this. Soon after prayer we heard protesters shouting in the street so we ran to the gate of the club to see what was happening. There were hundreds of protesters marching down the street, and the security men at the gate were warning everybody to stay inside. Without saying a word, the young teacher slipped out of the gate and disappeared into the street. I thought she was just trying to get a closer look. But then I could not see her. I stepped out of the gate and looked down the street. She was walking with the demonstrators further away, so I ran to her and insisted she come back to the club with me. On the way I apologized to her for intervening, explaining I could not take any chances and I could not take the responsibility. It was weird; it was like she was in some kind of trance, like a magnet being pulled. When we got back, she thanked me for bringing her back.

2pm, 3pm, 4pm... and my husband and son did not show up at the meeting point. I had been watching a television set near the table-tennis hall, which was broadcasting live. Things didn't look good. The police were attacking demonstrators with sticks, tear gas and high-pressure water. The scenes looked chaotic with people running, police vehicles driving all over the place and things burning. I was scared.

When the men didn't show up at 5pm, I decided to take our daughters to my in-laws' house, which would be safe. Then I went straight back to the club and watched the television. The army was now involved. They were on the streets and all hell could break loose! I was now panicking, silently crying and imagining the worst. Then there was an announcement that a curfew would start at 6pm. That was in about 45 minutes. At 5.58pm, I decided I had to leave, I didn't think my men would show up now anyway. I drove my husband's car to my in-laws'. At this point I was in very bad shape. In the privacy of the car I could sob properly, and I did. But as I approached the house I couldn't believe my eyes! My husband was there, alive and well. When we got into the house and I saw my son, I couldn't help it: I hugged them both and cried. I was so relieved.

We needed to hurry if we still wanted to make it home; the situation was deteriorating very rapidly on the streets. We promised my parents-in-law that if it were too dangerous we would turn back and spend the night with them. The streets looked like a war zone. It was dark. Cars and police vehicles and tires were on fire. There were stones and glass on the street. People and cars were going in all directions. Gunshots could be heard. Some streets were blocked by barricades that people had erected to protect themselves from the riot police. Other streets were blocked by army tanks. We kept on having to backtrack and try new roads that would hopefully get us home.

At one point we reached a group of men who were in the process of setting up a barricade. They were using barrels, tree trunks, big rocks and other material. As we drove past we gave them a cheer. A little way down, the road was blocked with a huge army tank. We turned around and drove back towards the barricade that had just been completed. When the men saw us they quickly made an opening to let us through and closed it again. We thanked them and encouraged them, and told them we were praying for them. They told us to stay safe.

About 50 meters ahead we saw a large number of riot police lined up, looking quite menacing ... were they going to attack these good men who had just let us through? My eldest daughter started crying, not because she was scared, but because it felt so horrible that we were fleeing in our cars to get home safely and were leaving those people on the street, possibly to fight for their lives. I felt so guilty! I was so angry; I didn't know what to do, everything was happening so fast. I tried to rationalize it to myself and to my daughter: *it's not as if we have done nothing, we've made banners and prepared the anti-teargas remedies. Your father and brother took part in the demonstration today and...* this wasn't working. She was inconsolable. I had to concentrate on driving. There was no order on the street. It was chaotic.

We got onto a bridge. Many people were walking. We saw some women and stopped to ask if anybody needed a lift. We took a young woman with us. My husband picked up three men. A few meters ahead there was a line of riot police blocking the bridge and shooting tear gas at people in front of them. I rolled down the window and screamed at one of them as I passed him, "These are your own people!" He waved his stick at me and told me to shut up and get out of there. Right there was an exit off the bridge. We took it and ended up back near where my parents-in-law live. We couldn't get home.

The young lady we picked up was a journalist. She had left her three-year-old son with her parents that morning. She said she couldn't just sit at home; she had to participate and cover the event. She lived quite far away. She hugged my daughter and tried to comfort her. I tried to convince her to spend the night with us and promised to take her home in the morning. I really felt it was much too dangerous for her, especially as she was on her own. But she refused to stay. The phone lines were down and she said she had to get back to her son, and her parents would be worried sick about her. She said she wasn't afraid at all, on the contrary, she felt very happy and she was at peace. We reached my in-laws' house; I drove up next to my husband's car and told him I would drive the lady home. He asked me to take the children inside and he drove her home himself, returning soon after.

When we got inside, we watched the television news, which showed the building of the ruling party on fire and people walking out with stolen chairs, lamps and other loot. They were not camera-shy at all. I think they figured they had a right because we had been ripped off for so many years and this stuff was bought with our money.

The sound of gunfire kept me up almost all night.

Saturday, January 29th: We went home in the morning. On the way we saw several burnt-out cars, some of them still smouldering. One of them was on the Qasr el-Nil Bridge, it was a police vehicle. That's probably the one my husband and son told us the police set on fire to have the excuse to attack the demonstrators, I thought. The National Democratic Party building was still on fire. How come we couldn't see any fire engines? There were a few tourists on the bridge taking photographs. They'd have a lot to talk about when they got home—certainly a different kind of holiday. There were people making their way to Tahrir Square. We drove on.

It was the end of the month and people hadn't been paid their salaries yet. Hatem and I decided to buy food and take it to Tahrir Square. My son was exhausted; he said he would not join us this time. My older daughter volunteered to do some housework and fix lunch, and my youngest came along. We took 200 sandwiches. But there were way more than 200 people there. It was weird seeing many of them standing on army tanks parked in the square. The soldiers were nowhere to be seen. Perhaps they were inside the tanks. The shops around the square were all closed. You couldn't even buy a bottle of water. We decided we'd have to go back and get more sandwiches and a big supply of water. But first we used the plastic bags we had brought the sandwiches in as garbage bags and started cleaning the garden in the center of the square. We had seen a man sweeping around the square and that gave us the idea. Several people joined us and the garden was soon clean.

When we got back after our second round of distributing food and water, we were not prepared for what we saw: the men of the neighborhood were in the streets holding sticks and knives, and one even held an axe. Some 17,000 prisoners had escaped from jail (or, as we later heard, had been set free) and the rumor was they were robbing stores and houses, and some were headed in our direction. What? This wasn't happening! They had also attacked our district's police station, stolen the weapons and set it on fire. We quickly went upstairs and got to work. In about an hour it would be dark and we had to be ready. We moved the fridge in front of the kitchen door. We moved the bookshelf in front of one of the entrances. The two younger children took buckets and collected rocks from next door where they were building a house and we put them on the balcony; we would throw them at the robbers if they got this far. We found gasoline at a neighbor's and we filled glass bottles a third of the way and inserted cloth into them, leaving a little sticking out on the top. This would be our last resort. Big iron structures had been made the day before on the construction site next to us, so those were moved to block the street. We happen to be the only apartment building on our very short, dead-end street.

This was all just too surreal.

I remembered my aunt. She lives alone on the ground floor in another district and her windows have no iron bars. We had to go get her. I called her. She sounded a bit shaken and I assured her that we'd come quickly. Hatem took our driver with him. They collected my aunt and dropped her off at another relative's house, returning safely.

Now my husband and son went down armed with a baton I had inherited from my grandfather, who used to be in the army, and a Taser [electroshock weapon]. Neighbors came up with all kinds of weapons: huge knives I thought only butchers used, swords, Tasers, canes and other big sticks, axes and licensed guns and rifles. Checkpoints were set up every 100 meters or so and any car that wanted to pass had to show identification, a driver's license and car papers to make sure it wasn't stolen; the driver had to have a really good reason for wanting to pass. Motorcyclists were dealt with very suspiciously. It was said the thugs often sent in one of those to check out the situation first.

Our men and boys were out there all through the night and all day guarding our neighborhoods all around the country. This continued for about ten days. The girls were anxious so they stayed up till very late but then were able to sleep on that first, totally freaky night. I couldn't, though; I stayed glued to the television watching the news next to the window. From my house I have a very good view of parts of three streets. I could see a couple of checkpoints and the groups of men guarding them, and every once in a while I'd see an army tank passing by. They're so loud you can hear them long before you can see them. They were there to help guard because the police had completely disappeared for some reason. It was as if they had just evaporated into thin air. When a thug was caught he was to be given in to the soldiers. Their presence reassured us a little.

I was so worried about those men out there; anybody could just come in shooting at any time. We didn't know if those criminals were attacking as individuals or in groups, and with what kind of weapons or vehicles. Every little while you'd hear shooting in the distance or quite close. You'd hear the men banging on metal sheets and whistling and shouting to signal danger to the others, and all of a sudden they would run towards one of the checkpoints. It was quite scary. It was very tense and it was very cold.

The phone lines had returned earlier that day, so everybody was calling everybody all through the night to make sure they were okay. We started being told by family and friends about incidents in different parts of Cairo and in Alexandria that were happening to them or to their loved ones. A lot of violence, looting and killing was going on. The reports came in on television as well. We couldn't believe we were in this situation. These things happened to other people, on CNN or in the movies.

Sunday, January 30th: Nobody went to work. In fact, nobody went to work that whole week. Everybody was concentrating on stocking up enough food to last at least a week. We had to do that, too. The shops were already out of a lot of things. One of the supermarket staff told my husband they would probably not be restocking any time soon, as they were afraid thugs would jump the trucks. What a mess!

That day we were on the phone a lot of the time, too. My son found out his schoolteacher was in hospital. He had been shot in the leg on the Friday. The doctor operated on him for eight hours. The bullet he removed was one that is internationally banned. When it enters the body it explodes and causes incredible damage. As a fellow demonstrator was carrying him away, he was shot with a weapon that emits tens of tiny pellets that filled his back and the back of his thighs with lots of small holes. He was in bad shape.

We got many phone calls from friends all over the world as well. It was really sweet of them, they were all so concerned. We kept hearing more and more stories about the thugs. Here are a few of them:

• My parents live together with my sisters and their families in a three-storey house. They told us that during the previous night a man drove through one of their checkpoints with a stolen police car, shooting randomly. He shot and killed a young boy in the process. The men at the checkpoint managed to catch him and took him into a building. At this point, my dad and brother-in-law, who had been outside, did not go into the building, so they don't know what they did with the man.

• A little earlier they had tied two suspicious men to a tree until they could deliver them to the soldiers.

• An old university friend who lives in Miami told us that the jewelry shop in his parents' apartment building in Alexandria was looted. His sister, who also lives in Alexandria, told him a bus with thugs was driving down their street, stopping at each apartment building and ringing the intercom telling people to send down their money and jewelry, or else they would come up.

Monday, January 31st: I wanted to go with Hatem to Tahrir. He said he would first have to call his cousin, who is a police officer, to ask what kind of orders they were being given and what the army's stance was. He didn't reach him until the afternoon. The police were busy catching the 17,000 prisoners and Hatem's cousin was guarding a big ammunition warehouse that had enough weapons to kill "two million people". They were not engaging with the protesters. It's true, you only saw army personnel on the streets. There weren't even traffic police, so civilians, bless their hearts, made it their job to keep the order. But what about the army? Could they attack? No, they had strict orders not to touch us. *Good*, I thought, *then I'm going tomorrow.*

All day I flipped through different television news channels. The people had occupied Tahrir Square and were not going to leave until Mubarak left. More and more reports came in about looting, even incidents of rape. The Carrefour in Alexandria that my mom and I had visited the previous week was empty; its branch in Cairo was empty as well. A friend of ours passed by there and said the only things that were not stolen were the walls. We heard that young teenagers armed with swords were stopping cars on the ring road around Cairo demanding money, mobile phones and jewelry, or else. The airport and the roads leading to it were jammed with foreigners and Egyptians fleeing the country.

Tuesday, February 1st: I left for Tahrir around noon with my husband. It was lucky that the revolution was taking place in the winter, as in the summer it would have been tortuous—at noon I might have got sunstroke! This time things looked different at the square. About 50 meters in front of it a checkpoint had been set up. You had to stand in a long line. Then you had to show your ID. They weren't police or army personnel at work at the checkpoint, just normal civilians. Anyone could volunteer to help out. If you were a policeman or a member of the National Democratic Party you were not allowed in. My rucksack was checked very thoroughly. Then I was body-frisked. Somebody else checked my bag once more. I was frisked a second time, and then a third time. I figured it must be my *niqab*, as everybody else was checked just once. But I didn't mind. On the contrary, I welcomed the process, especially since all of them were so polite and friendly, even apologetic. It was for all of our good.

The square was packed. We could not get inside. We sat on the sidewalk where it was not quite so crowded. It was beautiful. People from all walks of life were there. Children, students, middle-aged people, older people, Muslims, Christians, businessmen, laborers, foreigners, press people, the rich and the poor, people from Cairo and from other governorates [Egypt has 29 governorates or administrative areas] ... everybody was there. It was truly an uprising of the people.

That evening, we waited a long time for the president to speak. He spoke late that night. He said he would not run again, that he would work towards democratic elections in September, that he would make changes in the ministries and that he would work on all our requests. To be honest, I bought it. I figured he'd met pretty much all of our demands, most important of which was that we were not going to be stuck with him forever. I decided we should give him a chance. In addition to this I thought of all those people who had not yet been paid. The banks were closed and the economy was at a standstill. Also, a significant portion of our population consists of casual laborers. These people do not have much in terms of savings and for them it's a matter of survival. How were they to feed their families? Already eight people had died in bread lines, which is unforgivable. Hatem felt the same way. We were not going to go to Tahrir the next day.

By now the men in the neighborhood had organized themselves into shifts as you couldn't have all the men out like the first night. There was still the threat of robbers, but everybody was starting to get exhausted—guarding our homes at night, demonstrating during the day. Some had to be at the checkpoints during the day as well. Even when it was not Hatem's turn to guard for a few hours, we stayed up pretty much all night. The alarms could go off at any time and the men had to run down; they couldn't get too comfortable.

Wednesday, February 2nd: When I saw horses and camels galloping into Tahrir Square, I thought I wasn't seeing straight. I consider this day to be the climax of our revolution. We had decided we should pay my parents and parents-in-law a visit. The traffic was light on the way to my parents' house. There was just a small bottleneck next to the presidential palace. Several tanks guarded the building and they only let one car through at a time. My sisters and their families live in the same three-storey house so it was a good chance to see everybody.

On our way to my parents-in-law's the traffic was, again, light until we were about half way across the several-kilometers-long Sixth of October Bridge. Here, pro-Mubarak demonstrators were walking on the bridge, hindering traffic. They held banners, shouted slogans and stood in front of cars. You could honk your horn all you wanted, but you were either ignored or accommodated unhurriedly. They knocked on car windows and were just rude. They can have their own opinions, but they should have been civil like the demonstrators in Tahrir.

We moved very slowly. When we were at the part of the bridge overlooking Tahrir Square, we saw a bus parking with men sitting on the roof. When it stopped, the men quickly got off and out of the bus and, to our shock, they were carrying sticks and stones, and they were running towards the square. Ten minutes later, we arrived at my parents-in-law. They had the television on and this is when we saw what looked like a scene from the Middle Ages. Men on horseback and camels entered Tahrir Square and attacked protesters wildly with whips and sticks. They didn't make it very far. The demonstrators managed to pull them down. Some were beaten, understandably, and they were handed over to the army. Now war had started. The thugs attacked the demonstrators. They beat them with their sticks and threw stones, and chaos erupted. My mother-in-law said we should stay the night, but we wanted to give driving home a try; if we couldn't make it, we'd be back. We took an alternate route and thankfully made it.

As the whole world knows, things deteriorated terribly in Tahrir that evening. Demonstrators were fighting for their lives again. They threw Molotov cocktails at each other on the ground and from the rooftops. My daughter's 19-year-old classmate died that day. He was shot. She was in shock. A lot of people lost their lives that day. The prime minister denounced what had happened and so did the vice-president. They claimed to have no idea how all this came about and vowed to punish those responsible severely. Could we believe them? Could we take their promises seriously?

Thursday, February 3rd: Today a friend of ours set out from Heliopolis, a suburb of Cairo, with a very large group of demonstrators bound for Tahrir. It is about a 13km walk. When they were almost there, they were met by armed thugs who threatened to attack them if they advanced any further. They turned back. That same morning my son's sheikh [religious instructor] was beaten up as he was making his way to Tahrir. Thank God, he was all right.

I was already starting to question my decision to stay away from the protests and give the new government a chance. The day before yesterday, I was sure. Today, I wasn't so sure. Too many people were dying. I had watched an interview with the prime

Tahrir Square demonstrators spanned all classes, generations and religions

minister the day before and I was impressed. I had watched an interview with the vice-president and was not impressed at all. I decided to wait.

Friday, February 4th: I got a call from a German friend of mine in Cairo asking for permission to give my number to a ZDF journalist in Germany who wanted to talk to somebody who had been involved in the demonstrations. I agreed. She called and we talked for about half an hour.

Saturday, February 5th: Today and the next few days were peaceful in Tahrir. The army was protecting the demonstrators. They were still determined not to leave until he leaves. I had time to catch up on some sleep, watch a lot of news and think.

On Sunday, Hatem and the rest of the work force went back to their jobs. The banks were open again. After work my husband went to Tahrir for a while. It was like a small city now. There were places to spend the night: tents were set up and rooms were made simply from wooden rods with cotton sheets tied between them to form the walls and then plastic sheets (donated from a plastics factory) made the roofs. There were stands selling water, simple foods, cigarettes and even popcorn. Cabins were available with toilets. Doctors providing first aid were stationed in different places around the square. Stages were set up with big speakers where people could speak their mind, sing and even perform comedy sketches. There was a barber who offered his services for free. Blankets were donated and all kinds of free food and drink were distributed. These people were united, and prepared to stay for as long as it would take.

On Monday, I decided it was time for me to go back to Tahrir. The lives of all those who had died could not be in vain. If my husband or one of my children had been one of the dead, would I have stayed home? Definitely not! I also decided I did not trust the government. More and more reports of corruption and money laundering surfaced. It was quite clear now that the government had let out the prisoners and paid the different thugs on foot, on camel and on horseback to cause as much chaos and terror as possible. That president had to go. All his friends had to go, too. I went to Tahrir Square the next day.

Tuesday, February 8th: My sister and her friend came to Tahrir with me. My husband was still at work and would join me after. We went through the checkpoints—this time there were two. We made it into the square. It was crowded but would become more crowded later when people came after finishing work. The first thing that struck me was the number of banners with the photos of the "martyrs" that were hanging all over the place. Most of them were so young. One was a 10-year-old boy who was there the previous Wednesday during the so-called Battle of the Camels. He was shot.

We met a larger group of friends. It's hard to describe the atmosphere. It was a mix of excitement, a sense of unity, happiness and pride that we were, at last, standing up for our rights along with sadness for those who were injured or dead. There was also anger and determination, and, for the first time for me, true patriotism. It was wonderful! We felt very strong. We no longer felt suppressed and weak. We had a voice, and a very loud one, too. We chanted and chanted. He was going to hear us and he was going to surrender, he had no choice—we were going to win!

Wednesday, February 9th: My younger daughter and my son came to Tahrir with me this time. They hadn't been to school since January 27th. They go to an American school and many of their teachers had left the country. My older daughter attends the German University and many of its professors had departed, too. There was no word yet on when the schools and universities would reopen. My older daughter volunteered to do the housework. If she hadn't, we would have been coming home from the demonstrations to a chaotic house, no hot meals and an ever-growing mountain of laundry.

We met other girls from my younger daughter's class in Tahrir that day along with their siblings and moms. We walked around waving our flags and chanting with different groups of people. It was very exciting for the children. The children and I then found the perfect spot: it was in the middle of the square. We stood on an elevated area where it was not so crowded. The view was breathtaking. In every direction and as far as you could see, there were people: so many people! We started chants of our own. One of the girls or boys would say one and the rest of us would repeat in unison. We chanted as loud as we could. Soon people gathered around us and chanted along. Then a man with a drum joined us. More and more people gathered… soon we had a big following. The children loved it. I loved it. We went at it for over an hour.

My husband called me. There were rumors that thugs were on their way to Tahrir Square so he told us to get out of there immediately. We did. It was a false alarm.

Thursday, February 10th: Some friends I met on Tuesday told me that going to Tahrir had become addictive; if you didn't go one day you felt something was missing. I felt this, too. I couldn't not go. More and more people were joining. Thousands of doctors were marching from their syndicate towards Tahrir. It was a pretty sight; they all had their white coats on. Another march by lawyers also started. The previous day, teachers had been the first to march as a professional body.

I drove towards the square with my son. About half-way there, I got a phone call from my mother asking where I was. Alarmed, she told me to turn back. Companies were sending their employees home early. My mother said something was "brewing" and it was much too dangerous to go to Tahrir now. Tomorrow, Friday, was to witness the biggest demonstration yet. It looked like the government had something serious up its sleeve. My son and I were very disappointed. As I started back I called my husband. He said he would go anyway, but that we had to go home.

Mubarak was supposed to be giving a speech that evening. The international press were predicting he would stand down. US President Barack Obama's consultants were pretty sure about this. Our army claimed that the people would be getting all that they were asking for and that Mubarak would say something that would make us all very happy. Hatem said the atmosphere in Tahrir was one of joy and celebration. There was singing and dancing, and jumping up and down. I was so sorry I wasn't there. I watched the events at the square from home. I waited for the speech.

Mubarak came on. A few sentences into the speech, he said he promised to severely punish those responsible for the death of all those martyrs… what?! This meant he wasn't leaving! My heart almost stopped. The rest of what he said was so antagonizing, patronizing, arrogant, disappointing, horrible—just horrendous!

I really could not believe what I had just heard. I don't remember ever being so angry. My chest hurt and I was shaking. I was just too angry. I was speechless. I tried to breathe deeply to relax myself. I could not sit down, I was so tense. The reaction in Tahrir Square reflected what I was feeling; the roar was loud and powerful. The people interviewed were ready to die. "We'll show him what we're made of!" I thought: *Is he that much out of touch? Does he really not understand? Is he that glued to his chair?* The demonstrators were furious: "We're not leaving! We'll march to your palace tomorrow! We'll turn up by the millions tomorrow! You'll have to kill us all to stay!" Tons of phone calls went back and forth. Everybody was outraged. Everybody was going to be on the streets tomorrow.

Friday, February 11th: My husband left early with a friend to get into Tahrir Square in time for Friday prayers. He said we could not go yet. He had to check whether it was safe enough. I did not like that at all, but I was not going to argue. Everybody was stressed enough.

I stayed glued to the television. Some people were on their way to the presidential palace. That was very risky. My husband's police-officer cousin had told him once that if people got close enough to the palace, they'd get shot. I was so afraid for all of my brothers and sisters out there. The thing is, I had never before felt a part of the people of this country. I didn't belong to any country before; not Egypt, not Germany, not America. A new emotion was born inside me. Now I know what "patriotic" means. For me, that morning, it meant I was worried sick about my people in Tahrir, my people in front of the Television Building and *my* people already at—and on their way to—the presidential palace. I wanted to be with them so badly. I wanted to protect them from any harm. I was so restless. My phone rang. It was my husband. He said it was perfectly safe to go.

Yes! I was overjoyed! My son and younger daughter wanted to come along. My older daughter would come later. We got dressed in one and a half seconds and jumped into the car. We parked. As we got out of the car, a man sitting in front of his shop looked at me and muttered that all people in Tahrir Square should be clobbered with shoes. I thanked him and walked on. I noticed my son was not with us. I looked back and found him talking to the man. I quickly went over. My son couldn't handle his mom being insulted. I pulled him away and explained to the gentleman that everybody was entitled to their opinion but that one had to be respectful.

We had mastered respect and peace from our side for 18 days of the revolution so far. Were we not going to be able to apply that to our dealings with one another?   —*Mona Rushdy*

I was born in Egypt but I have an American passport. I took part in the protests for the first time on January 28ᵗʰ, Friday of Rage. I went with my father to the Mustafa Mahmoud Mosque for Friday prayers and met a friend of my father's. Afterwards, we were headed for Tahrir Square in downtown Cairo. My first impression of the revolution came as the imam finished the prayer and a man called out, "The People Want to Topple the Regime!" We started marching from the mosque, Christians, Muslims, atheists, you name it. We marched as one. We marched through Gamet el-Dowal Street and turned into el-Batal Ahmad Abdel-Aziz Street. We chanted "Silmeyya!" which means "Peaceful!", and to those watching us out of their windows we called out, "Ya Ahaleena Indammo Leena!" which means, "Our people, Come and Join Us!" We also chanted, "Gamal, Tell Your Father [Mubarak] the Egyptian People Hate Him!" There was an incredible sense of unity. We all helped each other—if someone was thirsty, we gave them water, things like that. I remember that on January the 28ᵗʰ, I felt national pride for the very first time. I felt that for the first time I could boast about being an Egyptian.

So we continued our march into al-Tahrir Street, where we met our first obstacle. At the end of the street, right before the first bridge leading into Tahrir Square, we were bombarded with tear gas, even though our chants of peace had not ceased. The tear gas was so painful that some men fell over and could not get up again. We fought the tear gas by using towels and tissues soaked with vinegar, which we inhaled. We also poured fizzy drinks into our eyes to stop them burning.

I saw the riot-control officers set fire to one of their own cars, and I also saw a flaming tear-gas canister go into a house and set it on fire. It was an appalling scene. We were able to make headway after an hour or so. By that time, the riot-control officers had fled in one of their trucks. We deflated the other trucks' tires so that they could not be used again, but we did not wreck them. Later, when we returned, I saw the trucks being wrecked. We reached the second barrier in front of the Opera House, and passed through without much struggle. We continued our march towards Tahrir Square.

We went onto the Qasr el-Nil Bridge where we almost broke the barrier, and then the riot-control people started treating us civilians in ways I could not imagine them treating animals. They started firing explosive bullets at us, and every few minutes someone would come out of the crowd bleeding or close to death. I saw a man with a bandaged head who was standing strong and was going back in for more. They also started driving over people, and we could see the personnel carriers going up and down as if driving over speed bumps. We had to retreat, there was no other choice for us, and we retreated all the way back to the square at the Opera House. By that time I was getting dizzy, so we sat down for a couple of minutes and then got back up to continue to demand our rights. What amazed me most that day was that we weren't only Egyptians in the protests. I saw a couple of foreign teachers from my school, and we asked why they had come. One of them said: "For humanity." He also said that he did it to help his Muslim brothers.

On Saturday morning I was so tired I could not help my family give out food and drink at Tahrir Square. I went later that afternoon, however, and helped distribute more refreshment. It was very crowded and people were eager for whatever little food we could bring them, as many had been in the square for a day or more. We turned to go back home before the curfew started. That night, and the one before that, were the two most violent nights of the revolution. Although I would have given up anything to stay there, we could see on the news how brutal the police force could be, and how the army was taking a neutral stance.

Then came the Wednesday known as the Day of the Camel, when the government sent bullies to try to force the people to leave Tahrir Square. They came on camels and horses with swords and knives, whips and occasionally even guns. I wasn't in the battle, but I wanted to be. Some of the stories I heard made me regret not being there. There was this man, for example, who was hit in the head; he went and got six stitches, then came back for more. He got another blow to the head and got nine stitches, and still came back for more. Then he got another blow worthy of even more stitches, and still he came back for more. He then got a bullet to the shoulder, and he was crying because he couldn't go back for more. Before we had evidence that these pro-Mubarak bullies were government organized, we thought they were just some men who wanted to create trouble. But then after the horse and camel riders were beaten up, they confessed that they had been paid to come and do this. Some say that it was the Muslim Brotherhood and the hardcore Ahly and Zamalek football-club fans who had repelled the bullies, but I think it was a mix of those and the rest of the people in Tahrir Square.

The next week flew by very quickly with million-man marches on Friday, Sunday, and Tuesday. During these marches, you couldn't see the ground, there were so many people. It was a week of strange happenings. First, the government opened up the prisons and freed all the convicts, so we had to protect our houses and neighbors. I would guard the house for most of the day and a few hours at night. We would constantly hear about ex-convicts or new burglars and thieves being caught, but no action ever reached our street.

On Thursday night, the president was going to give a speech, and everyone expected him to step down. There was a celebratory atmosphere all around Cairo, and I'm sure the rest of Egypt as well. The speech, however, was a shock to everybody, even the foreign news agencies and the CIA, who all expected Mubarak to resign. He did not resign, but instead handed most of his powers to Vice-President Omar Suleiman, whom most people did not like nor approve of.   —*Ziyad Rushdy*

POLICEMEN, TELL THE TRUTH:
ARE WE NOT YOUR BROTHERS?

Mohamed Aziz

Mohamed Aziz, 26, is a human resources executive with Ezz Steel Manufacturing. Despite working for a company that benefited from close ties to the regime, joining the demonstrations was a natural impulse for Mr. Aziz. Along with many, he experienced being gassed and beaten during Friday of Rage. He describes how neighborhood vigilante teams were formed during the revolution.

~

I was sitting with some friends at a coffee shop on Thursday, January the 27th, and we started talking about Friday, the next day, and wondering what it would be like. Would the police be violent? Then one of my friends, who works at Vodafone, got a phone call and told us that the government had ordered the text messaging service on our phones to be shut down—starting now. So we tried sending messages to each other to check and found that they weren't being delivered, even though we got a delivery report. A while afterwards, I got a BlackBerry message about the meeting points where the demonstrations would start. The list included all big mosques and churches in Cairo. Then the Internet stopped working. No service on BlackBerry, no Internet, no messages. We talked some more about who wanted to go down to the streets the next day, and who didn't. Some were scared and some needed encouragement. Anyway, I said I would be going, so they told me I was short-tempered and liked a fight. I didn't care what they said, and I told them I was going anyway.

So the next day, I prayed at the mosque under my parents' house in Giza on Mourad Street and ran quickly to Giza Square to al-Istiqama Mosque because it was one of the meeting points mentioned in the BlackBerry message. Central Security forces had set up three barricades of paramilitaries and cars around the mosque, so that if the demonstrators got through the first one, they would be stopped by the second, and if they got through the second, they would be blocked by the third. Manning these barricades were tens or maybe hundreds of policemen from Central Security.

When I got to the mosque, the prayers hadn't finished and the police wouldn't let me in. As soon as the prayers were finished at al-Istiqama Mosque, people started yelling "Allahu Akbar!" (God is Great) and other slogans which were very beautiful and motivating. Then I found a whole group of demonstrators coming from el-Gamea Street, so I ran and joined them and I went into the middle of the crowd. There were all kinds of people, some well-heeled, others looking a bit poorer. But they all seemed on the same side. We started shouting: "The People Want to Topple the Regime!" and "Ministry of Interior Policemen, Tell the Truth: Are We Not Your Brothers?" and "Freedom, Freedom!" and other slogans.

We managed to join the people at the mosque and we became one big group of demonstrators. Then suddenly I spotted that there were fire engines behind the paramilitary police and they were beginning to move forwards, almost pushing the police into the crowd of demonstrators. It seemed strange, almost like the fire engines were forcing the security police to start beating us. Thank God, I wasn't in the front lines because these guys got the worst beatings. The fire engines opened their water pumps on us to separate us, and then the tear gas came, like crazy—they fired tons of tear gas at us. People were choking and crying from the tear gas, but we were still shouting out our slogans. I was a bit scared, but when I found many other people still standing, my heart grew stronger and I thought to myself, none of these people is better or braver than me.

Then the beating really started with these big wooden sticks they carry. The police were hitting us with viciousness, as if we had stolen their money or taken their land or something, it was beyond my comprehension. They were beating us with anger, fury, very viciously. We got separated into smaller groups and suddenly there were many people coming from the houses around us onto the streets and helping us. Some people took the tear-gas bombs and threw them into the security police's trucks. The canisters were being shot so randomly, one of them went on to the roof of a building in Giza Square and caught fire.

I pushed a policeman, then I ran home to wash my face as I really couldn't see because of the tear gas. Then I went back down onto the street to see that the police were retreating. People started burning their trucks, so I went back home because I was worried by the burning of the vehicles. When I went out a while later, I found the people venting their fury and taking out their oppression on the police cars. I felt worried.

I went back up to my house and started watching television to see what was going on everywhere else. There was a report that thieves and burglars were everywhere. I heard a call from the mosque near our house asking all the men to go down to the street because there were a lot of strangers in the neighborhood. My mother started crying, afraid for me, and begging me not to take the knife. She was worried I might kill someone and get into trouble. I told her there were some criminals in the street and if I didn't go down they would sooner or later come up here and kill us or rob our house. I took a stick and a knife and went down.

On the stairs I met my neighbor, a young Christian guy who is quite slightly built, so I was worried he might not be able to take care of himself. So I told his mother not to let him down onto the street alone, and that he could only go down with me. I took him with me and, together with others who had gathered, we set up a checkpoint at each end of our street. We took a broken-down minibus and pushed it into the middle of the street to block it. We did not let anyone through until we had checked their ID, and if they were not from our neighborhood or if they were police officers we did not let them through. Also, if it was someone we didn't know, we would check their trunks and their cars for any weapons. There were a lot of rumors that criminals would seize this time of chaos to go looting.

While we were standing in the street, a taxi came towards us. We stopped it and asked to see the driver's license and the passenger's ID. So the driver showed us his license and that was all fine, and as we were checking the trunk, the passenger said he was a police officer and pulled out a gun. We threw ourselves onto him, not giving him a chance to fire it, and some people took the fire extinguisher from the taxi's trunk and sprayed him with it. One man had a stun gun and started giving him electric shocks. We pulled him out of the car and we were all choking because of the white spray that came out of the fire extinguisher, but the people who were outside were fine so they started beating him up after taking the gun from him. Then after he was completely beaten up, almost dead really, we took him to the army patrol car that was at the end of our street. We told the army officer that the guy said he was a policeman and handed over the gun we took from him. The army officer said to us, "The police can go f--k themselves; the army is in charge now."

On another day, my wife and I had to go out in the evening and I was stopped at several of these checkpoints formed by the people—we were calling them "legan sha'beya" (public committees). And some of them were very decent and didn't even ask to see any ID, I assume because I'm obviously not a criminal and I had my wife with me. But some of them were extremely aggressive and almost scary, waving their knives in my face and talking in the same rude way the police used to talk before. I guess there are good and bad people everywhere.

PEOPLE DIED IN FRONT OF MY EYES

Fadel Soliman

Fadel Soliman, 45, is the chairman of the Bridges Foundation, a non-profit organization that aims to unite people from different religious and ethnic backgrounds through educational interfaith activities. He was, for four years, the host of "The Islamic Show" on cable television in the United States, as well as a radio show entitled "Let the Quran Speak". Mr. Soliman is a former national swimming champion. He was the Muslim Chaplain at the American University in Washington, D.C. from 2001 to 2004.

~

A friend of mine told me on January 15th that Egypt would follow Tunisia within weeks. I disagreed with him, saying Egyptian people are too docile. He had more faith in the people than I did. And so on January 25th, I did not participate. It seemed to me that 500 Facebook guys protesting was not a real revolution. But the following day I started preparing myself. I sent emails to everyone I knew asking them to prepare themselves to say the truth. On the 27th I received a lot of calls from people I know asking me whether I thought they should join Friday of Rage. I told them it was a religious necessity ("fard ein") that every man go and a preference ("nafela") for every woman.

So on Friday, January 28th, I went to al-Nour Mosque in Abbasia, one of the meeting points. After the prayers were finished, we went out onto the street and stood outside the mosque. The Central Security forces started closing in on us and so we could not go anywhere except in the direction of el-Geish Street, calling people who were watching from their balconies to come down and join us. We grew in number to between five and seven thousand people. It was very peaceful and very beautiful. When we reached Bab el-Shereya, on our way to Tahrir Square, they started hitting us with the tear gas. We changed direction towards Ramses Street and onto Ramses Square, where they again started firing tear gas at us. They would hit us with the tear gas and we would retreat, and then go forward again, then they would fire it again and we would retreat and so forth.

I remember a scene when about 50 Central Security paramilitaries were surrounded by demonstrators behind a shop at the end of Ramses Street. These people had just been beating us and gassing us, yet the people who surrounded them, were in fact protecting them. They kept on yelling, "Selmeyya" (peaceful) and "El-Asaker la'a" (not the paramilitaries). And they kept insisting that nobody beat or attack the paramilitary officers [who assisted the Egyptian Police Force]. So really it was a peaceful and beautiful demonstration. Any violence was from the police force. Not only did they attack us with tear gas, they fired live ammunition as well. People died, people died in front of my eyes opposite the Azbakeya Police Station. The armored cars they use were driven by maniacs, running over people in front of us.

Then I got an idea. I thought maybe instead of retreating every time they fired the tear gas at us, I should try and break through to the other side. But I found out that the tear gas covered quite a distance; it must have been 50 meters not just five or six meters like I thought. I was choking and I was running with my eyes closed. It got too much and I fell down, unable to move and feeling like I was going to die. The devil whispered in my ear, "You have done enough, you have been hit four or five times with tear gas, at your age, this is enough, go home." As I was trying to get up to turn around and go home I saw a young woman, who works with me, accompanied by a group of friends. "Dr. Fadel," they said, "do you need vinegar, or Coca Cola, and do you need to sniff an onion?" As they said this, they were clearly preparing to move forward and push into Tahrir Square. The courage of these girls taught me a lesson I will never forget.

On the 29th, we started sleeping in Tahrir Square. We heard of the large numbers of martyrs who had died everywhere. January 30th and 31st and February 1nd were relatively normal days. I met a friend of mine who was there every day with his wife and two daughters, even in the middle of all this violence by the police.

Then on February 2nd, it was Bloody Wednesday, or the Day of the Camel. On that day, my wife and children insisted on joining me. I was a little late leaving the house because of that and so by the time we were about to leave, the camels and horses sent by the National Democratic Party had already started attacking the demonstrators in Tahrir. I got a call from someone in Tahrir telling me that the situation was very bloody, and that I should not go there now. Instead, I should call someone in the police force. I have some connections and so I called one of them, saying, "Our sons and daughters are being slaughtered in Tahrir!" I was saddened and shocked to hear him say, "Let them get slaughtered, what are they doing there in the first place?" I said, "You know very well what they are doing there, they have demands, and they are staying there to get their demands met." So he said, "Fine, let them get slaughtered for their demands." So I said, "The international community is watching us." He used dirty words (that I prefer not to repeat) about the whole of the international community. I replied by saying that the regime has signed its own death warrant today. He told me to get off the phone and go and watch Mehwar TV.

At that time on Mehwar, they had a girl being interviewed, who claimed that she had been trained by Jews in the United States to topple the regime. The interviewers were asking her what specifically she had received training in and she would respond, "toppling the regime". But what specific training did you get, and she would say, "Toppling the regime." Then the senior security official called me back asking what I thought of what I had just seen, and I said this would be very dangerous and serious talk if it weren't completely fabricated.

Anyway, I could not go down to Tahrir that day, because the

مقاتل فى حرب أكتوبر
يريد
إسقاط النظام

"An October War veteran wants to topple the regime."

The army was welcomed by demonstrators,
though it remained a neutral protector

road was blocked at that time. The next morning, I went back down to the Square and saw, with my own eyes the results of the massacre. Almost everyone I saw had some injury. The least hurt had blood all over their clothes and bandages wrapped round their heads. One of them was a friend of mine; he is one of the biggest businessmen in Egypt, owner of one of the most famous fast-food chains in the country. I messaged him recently telling him I am proud to be his friend.

One of the people who was with us during these days is the general manager of one the biggest banks in Egypt. I asked him how our economy would be affected. He said, "Fadel, if the regime is changed, the economy will boom, the biggest problem here is corruption. The main problem is that we lose a lot of money and there is a lot of capital outflow as a result of this corruption."

Friday the 4th was Departure Friday, the day we all thought would be the last in the regime's life. I remember there was a problem with who should give the Friday prayer sermon, whether it should be Sheikh Gamal Kotb, or the official imam of Omar Makram Mosque. Some people thought it should be Gamal Kotb; others thought it should be the government-appointed sheikh who should do it, because we want to respect the official appearance of this large mosque. My own view was that Sheikh Gamal should be the one to give it, but in the end, the official imam, called Mashar, gave the sermon. It was a wonderful sermon, inspirational and revolutionary and he invited the people to stay in Tahrir Square and assured them that what they were doing was completely "halal" and "shar'y" [religiously correct].

That night, Mubarak gave a sentimental speech, asking people that he stay until the end of his term, because he had given Egypt a lot, during times of peace and times of war. After the speech, I witnessed a split happening within the people's ranks. Before the speech, all the people I know were insisting that he leave immediately, but after the speech, the camp was split into two groups. One group was still insisting that he leave immediately and the other still wanted him to leave but was willing to wait until September. Some people in Tahrir started calling anyone who insisted on his immediate departure a traitor. They were saying, "Enough, we need to get back to work, he has promised to leave. What more do you want?" I remember I met a man after prayers the following morning, and he told me, "I am a day worker, I make ten pounds [about US$1.65] per day, and all the people in Tahrir are young people who get pocket money from their parents or rich business people." I said, "These young people who get pocket money from their parents and these wealthy business people don't need to demonstrate. They are doing it for you, so that you can make more than 10 pounds a day. You should join them instead of complaining about them."

That day I called Dr. Yusuf al-Qaradawi [a famous Muslim cleric in Egypt] and asked him to make a statement to the people who were dampening the fervor of the demonstrators in Tahrir and he did on Al Jazeera news channel. I believe it had a huge impact on the feelings of the people in Tahrir.

That same day, the UK's *Guardian* newspaper published its explosive article on the wealth and fortune of Mubarak and his family, saying that it was somewhere between US$40 and US$70 billion. I called Dr. Mohamed Selim el-Awa [a highly respected Islamic scholar and political activist] and Dr. Safwat Hegazy [an Islamic television figure and a very active man in Tahrir during the revolution]. I suggested to them that instead of asking for Mubarak to leave we should raise the bar and ask that he, his wife and family not be allowed to travel and to stay in Egypt to be tried in court. Then we could find out how he acquired this immense wealth. Maybe then he would just leave! They liked the idea and so I called the people who were leading the slogan-calling in the square and told them to start using slogans to this effect.

Despite Prime Minister Ahmed Mohamed Shafik's pledge that none of the demonstrators would be arrested for their actions, it seemed the phones were tapped and the very next morning a number of State Security officers arrived at my house in plain-clothes and in a regular car to arrest me. Fortunately, I was not there. So they went to my office, but our offices had been closed since the beginning of the demonstrations. But the doorman from my house—and a few minutes later the doorman from my office —called me and told me that these people had come for me.

On February the 6th, a Sunday, a million people came to Tahrir. So that people could go back to work and get on with their lives, we had discussed holding million-man marches on Sundays, Tuesdays and then Fridays. But what happened was that the revolution took on a momentum of its own, not only beyond the control of the government, but also beyond the control of organizers in Tahrir. There were strikes by government employees, factory workers and everybody else. Instead of getting a million people on Sundays, Tuesdays and Fridays, it looked as though we were getting a million people in Tahrir every day.

IT'S BIZARRE COMPARING WHAT I CAN SEE FROM MY FLAT WITH WHAT EGYPTIAN TELEVISION IS SHOWING

Pierre Sioufi

Born in 1961, Pierre Sioufi has acted both in theatre and in cinema, and he has also worked as a casting director. During the 18 days of the revolution, he had a unique view from his home on the top floor of a high-rise building directly overlooking Tahrir Square. Here are some of Mr. Sioufi's significant observations from a few of those days, which he shared at the time with the rest of the world via a real-time Facebook blog.

~

Friday, January 28th, 3pm: Listening to the tear gas being thrown at people trying to reach Tahrir Square. There is a big group of people in Talaat Harb Square. Another attack is being prepared to defend Bab el-Louk Square, where there is also a big group of protesters. I am wondering how they will keep their positions; the sound of the tear-gas bombs is an indicator that the security forces are attacking protesters from that side quite strongly, but then the protesters who were in front of the Opera House started walking through Qasr el-Nil Bridge and are having some success. They have been attacked with tear gas, but they keep advancing.

It is now a bit later. I have lost count of the number of tear-gas bombs that have been thrown. But the protesters are determined. I have watched between 20 and 30 people get arrested, but I haven't been keeping my eye on it all the time. The protesters' chanting floats up through the air, but far more noticeable is the sound of the salvos of tear gas. You would think you were in Iraq during the American attacks. Protesters have been pushed back from the square but are still holding positions in front of Metro cinema. Bab el-Louk is now back in the hands of security forces but they had to extend their defences; many arrests have happened there. Qasr el-Nil was full of protesters at one point, but they've been pushed back with water cannons and tear gas. It's bizarre comparing what I can see from my flat with what Egyptian television is showing. If you watch the news, the protesters have left the streets and things are back to normal. I wonder when the media censors will stop this counterproductive technique of hiding news. The risky decision by the government to block the Internet and mobile phone lines will harm the business community; they're already feeling the crunch.

8pm: Tahrir Square is still a battlefield. But there has been an announcement that the army is taking over the streets and a curfew has been imposed. The police look disoriented. Many have left in trucks. The most generous tear-gas salvo was sent towards Qasr el-Nil, while the police forces retreated. After the smoke dissipated, the protesters had a clear route, all the way to an empty Tahrir Square.

A little after midnight, the army came into the square. The curfew has not been implemented. The square is still full of protesters chanting and just standing around the army tanks.

Saturday, January 29th, 1.30am: A new salvo of tear gas is sent from somewhere beside the parliament building. The protesters have complained to the soldiers in the army tanks. A couple of the tanks left their positions in the square and repositioned in front of the forces of the Ministry of the Interior, thus defending the protesters.

2am: More tear-gas salvos.

4.20am: Shots and explosions are heard close by, but protesters are still standing in the square and chanting. The army is slowly getting out of the square, but protesters are still here. They are tired but, from time to time, a new round of chanting starts.

5am: The chants are still coming up from the streets and protesters still do not seem keen on going home, although the weather has turned cold.

Sunday, January 30th, 10am: Last night I went into the square twice. Everyone was exhausted and tempers were short. The army had been out on the streets for nearly 60 hours without a break and the protesters are very tired. The army has sent in fresh troops, who arrived this morning.

Monday, January 31st, 9.20am: A very hard night for the protesters. It was very cold. They had to walk around the square, sometimes even running in circles, chanting slogans, in order to warm themselves up. The numbers dwindled to a couple of thousand during the night, but are beginning to increase again this morning.

1pm: Some 40,000 are now in the square demonstrating. Whenever a helicopter passes overhead, the crowds cover the sound of it, chanting "Erhal!" (Leave!).

Wednesday, February 2nd: Men came into the square mounted on horses and camels, attacking the demonstrators. There's a war down there. It seems they were paid members of the National Democratic Party and government thugs. We have seen many injured protesters taken to the infirmary.

The numbers of protesters dwindled for a short time but then, in spite of at least one confirmed death and at least 50 to 60 injured, they regrouped.

Friday, February 4th: Protesters are on the street. They have come in great numbers. I would estimate there are about 700,000 and the roar of the crowds chanting is extraordinary. What a day this is!

Sunday, February 6th, 4am: The party is still happening through the night. Everything is fine. Up to now, there has been no attack. One wonders what is in store for tomorrow. Nothing much happened on the square on Saturday. But the regime is likely trying to rethink its image, and considering getting rid of some of the figureheads who are hated by the public. It has been raining and the night is cold. There is a call for another million-man march for today. The arm-wrestling is still on, it seems.

3.06pm: There is a huge number of people in the square—about half a million, although the entrances to the square have stringent security measures. The queue at the entrance on Qasr el-Nil Bridge goes at least as far as the new opera house. Many supporters bring in food supplies and blankets, and then go on with their daily lives.

1.33pm: Yet another funeral of the martyrs of the revolution passes through the square. This one is for Egyptian journalist Ahmad Mahmoud, who was shot in his office in the Al-Ahram building.

8pm: Some shots are fired, but they seem to be just a salvo by the army to reassure the demonstrators after some thugs tried to move the demonstrators' barricades. Other than this incident, there was a party atmosphere here all day. There was even a live concert in the square during the day. Some artists decided to come and paint the roads on the square. Woodstock on the Nile!

Monday, February 7th: Wael Ghoneim, the blogger who started the Facebook page "We are all Khaled Said", widely considered as the spark that began all of these protests, has been released from detention. [Khalid Said was a young Egyptian man who died in 2010 after being beaten by police.] There were rumors that Ghoneim would come to the square. He then sent out a Twitter message confirming his release but said he would not come to the square today.

Tuesday, February 8th, 10.08am: A slow night. An eerie night, actually. For the first time, it felt like people were sleeping. I believe protesters were exhausted and just crashed, since today might be hard because they had called for another million-man march. The logistics involved in such an event are complicated, especially for people who are exhausted and tense.

6.35pm: I wonder if occupation of the square is the right way to describe what is happening now. This is the biggest march we have had. There is news that the buildings of the Shura Council and the Council of Ministers are under siege, or at least cordoned off by demonstrators.

Wednesday, February 9th, 11.05pm: The protesters have succeeded in blocking the doors to the Parliament—a parliament in which more than two-thirds of members have used unlawful means to get elected.

Thursday, February 10th, 8.19pm: It's all a bit surreal; there have been celebrations in Tahrir Square all day. The celebrations started this morning. The square is bubbling with the sweet taste of victory, even though nothing has actually happened.

10.25pm: Everyone is sitting around radios or televisions waiting for victory. But, for some reason, I am pessimistic. I'm also worried that, even if Mubarak does step down, we'll get Mr. Sillyman, as he's now called [Vice-President Omar Suleiman], as a goodbye present.

11.05pm: I was right to be pessimistic. Mubarak doesn't understand at all. His hard-headedness is incredible. He should just take his pension and go. Is it so difficult to understand that the Egyptian people want to be proud of themselves again, to be free of all this brainwashing?

Thousands of protesters have gathered outside the radio and television building. The atmosphere is tense. The building is surrounded by tanks and barbed wire, with heavily armed soldiers. On several first-floor balconies, soldiers stand behind machine guns pointing toward the crowds.

The crowds are chanting, "Down With the Fraudulent Media! Down with the Fraudulent Broadcasters! Down with Mubarak!"

We also have news that many protesters have arrived at the presidential palace.

THE MOMENT HE QUIT

This book's contributors share their stories' conclusions at the time the revolution reached its climactic finale.

MANSOUR ABDEL GHAFFAR: I think what changed between Thursday and Friday was that he knew there was a ten-million-man march planned for that day. Many people had already decided to march to the presidential palace in Heliopolis; many had decided to take over the official radio and television station offices. I think this is when he decided he would leave. That night the vice-president came out and said that Mubarak had left the presidency. I cannot describe how happy I was when we heard that. I was overjoyed, it was indescribable joy. I am diabetic so I need to use the bathroom frequently, and when the actual announcement was made I was at the mosque using the facilities. When I came out, people were overjoyed. New chants were being called: "Al-Shaab Askat el-Nezam!" (The People Have Toppled the Regime!) and "Erfaa Rasak, Fa'enta Masry!" (Raise Your Head High, You're an Egyptian!).

I want to add that those days in Tahrir Square were days of amazing strength and courage. We had nothing but our faith in what we were doing. The enemy was well-trained, well-equipped, armed, while we had nothing. A new nation was born. People changed from within. We became stronger and more confident in ourselves. We really changed the country.

AZZA TAWFIK: This was the first time I cried in Tahrir since January 25th. We went to a side-street café that had a television to wait for the speech they had announced earlier. The minute Omar Suleiman said it, I stood on my chair, cheering, laughing... telephone calls, telephone calls... people who had struggled alongside me during the past two weeks, people who were still searching for their missing loved ones. Happiness, relief, hope, many feelings came out in hysterical tears the moment I returned to Tahrir Square from the café and looked up at the building where a huge banner hung with photos of the martyrs... I looked at each one of them and thanked them, wished they were there, felt them around, knew they were with us and happy with the achievement, the achievement they had paid for with their lives for us to see and live.

I cried out all the pain and the anger, I cried for the innocent faces smiling at us from the banner, and their families who will miss them forever. God bless them and may they rest in peace. They paid the price of Egypt's freedom.

"Hurriya!" (freedom) was the immediate cheer most people chanted. And then, for the first time: "Hold your head high, you are Egyptian!"

AMR WAKED: I was in the square when Mubarak made his speech on the last Thursday, February 10th, saying that he was not leaving. People were screaming, "You bastard, don't you understand the word LEAVE?"

One thing I really did not like at the time was the Egyptian satellite channels—not the official ones, because you expect those to walk the party line—but the so-called independent ones, which played dirty. They would present both points of view; the demonstrators' and the government's and then they would allow the government's viewpoint to seem more rational. It was the cheapest form of criticism, putting on the appearance of neutrality and honesty while clearly sending the message you want to anyway. You can accept and understand that from the state television, but the independents should do better. This was especially true after the speech where Mubarak handed over powers to his deputy Omar Suleiman; these television stations were again conspiring against the demonstrators, saying this is more than anybody expected, we are very lucky to get this much, you should all go home. Can you imagine, after all these efforts, the dead martyrs, after everything, they want us to go home based on some promises? They used all kinds of tactics to try to scare us: There would be economic destruction; there were foreign agents involved; creating fear of the Muslim Brotherhood—they used all manner of things. One of the saddest in my view was Al Jazeera Arabic which seemed to be inciting demonstrators to get more aggressive, and I didn't like that.

Then, of course, came the fantastic news that he was leaving, and honestly I can say that was the happiest moment of my life. We did it, man!

HATEM MO'MEN: I took my wife, children and brothers and went to the palace. One incident that happened that day was of great significance to me. We were at first a small number at the palace and I noticed an old woman in a nearby building peeking from behind her balcony shutters, watching the scene. We were calling our chants and asking for Mubarak to leave. This lady was in her house, almost hiding behind the shutters. Little by little, the number of people increased and she took half a step into the balcony. She was still clearly afraid to come out all the way onto the balcony but she was doing it little by little. She seemed to be almost driven by the number of people on the street. In the end, when Mubarak's resignation was announced, she came all the way out on the balcony, leaned over and cheered with the crowds. I could see, minute by minute, her fear barrier breaking down. It was amazing.

When the announcement was made, I took my wife and kids and we went to Tahrir Square to celebrate. Everybody was there, the demonstrators and the people who had stayed home. It was a battle that the demonstrators (or I should say, revolutionaries) had won, but all Egyptians celebrated the victory.

ISLAM MO'MEN: So sure enough the next day, which was a Friday, we prayed and then went to the palace. We were not obstructed at all, and the numbers grew very rapidly. Then came the final moment, when the vice-president announced that Mubarak was leaving. I put my flag down, knelt and prayed and I remembered all the people who had died in the past weeks, and I sobbed for a long time. These people had wanted to make a difference to their country. We now have to make sure their hopes don't die with them.

MONA RUSHDY: My husband Hatem and his friend had volunteered to man a Tahrir checkpoint. When my childen and I arrived at the square, he joined us. It was super-crowded. We stayed a while and then went home. I was thinking I should make more banners to take with me in the days to come. It didn't look like we were going to leave Tahrir any time soon.

In the early evening, we had dinner in front of the television. We couldn't miss out on anything. Suddenly, the vice-president came on. What now...? What?! Oh my God! He has resigned! This was too good to be true! Totally unexpected! Yes! Yes! Yes! We high-fived and hugged and kissed each other. We did it! We did it! It was unbelievable. We had been extremely angry just a few minutes ago. Now we were incredibly happy. I needed to concentrate for a few seconds to really let it sink in. I thought about the rollercoaster of emotions we'd all experienced in the last two short weeks. We had to go to Tahrir, right away!

The whole city was outside. The streets leading to the square were completely jammed. I had never, ever in my life thought that I would not only not mind a traffic jam, but actually enjoy it immensely! We leaned out of the windows and sat on the roof of the car, and waved our flags and honked like crazy! We parked and continued on foot with the crowds.

Everybody was ecstatic! We walked between the cars, we congratulated and hugged each other, and we sang and danced and watched fireworks. It was a sense of freedom, pride and victory that we all shared together. If we weren't talking or singing, we were just smiling. How many times had we said in the past years that the people in this country do not smile anymore? There was enough smiling that evening to last the next 20 years.

We had no leader in this revolution. Our dreams were our weapons.

ZIYAD RUSHDY: On Friday, February 11th, Mubarak stepped down. The statement was made by Suleiman, and it indicated that the president had already left. That was when our dreams came true, we were free, we stood up to the tyrant and told him to leave, that he was not wanted, that 30 years of dictatorship and tyranny were enough. They say one-third of Cairo's population took to the streets that day to celebrate. Celebrations were still being held on Friday, February 18th. During this revolution I felt for the first time like I could boast about being Egyptian, I felt real national pride.

FADEL SOLIMAN: Friday, February 11th, was Challenge Friday. I was invited to be a member of the committee that would write the statement by the people of the January 25th revolution. We were maybe 15 people, including some media personalities and several judges and other members of the judiciary. The group also included a Christian man, Ihab Aziz I believe his name was, and we wrote the statement and it was publicised.

That night, then-vice-president Omar Suleiman announced that Mubarak had given all his powers to the Higher Council of the Armed Forces, and that he was no longer the president of Egypt. My wife and children were driving to Tahrir so that we could all celebrate together and they passed in front of the Mubarak Police Academy and found the policemen there, ripping down any pictures of Mubarak.

PIERRE SIOUFI: The revolution has ousted a dictator and ended a dictatorial regime. I love it. I love it! I had moments of discouragement, but those kids were there fighting for their cause with a determination we rarely witness. They forced the police and their henchmen to retreat. It is true that they were helped by the fact that the uprising was happening all over Egypt and security forces were over-extended. Without the battles between security forces and the activists in Suez City and other towns, the revolution would have failed.

Now the revolution has succeeded in removing the dictator. Nevertheless, the situation remains unclear. What happens to all the figureheads of the regime? They need to be prosecuted under a fair and independent legal system that will give them a chance to present their case. The National Democratic Party must be disbanded. It is not so much a political party as a club of the same elite that has been ruling Egypt since the mid-1940s, under different names with different figureheads. If the president is a member of a party, then a condition of assuming the post must be that he resigns from the party. The presidency should be above party politics.

AMR BASSIOUNY: As I write this we continue to fight our revolution, though Hosni Mubarak has gone and the Supreme Council of the Armed Forces is in charge. They have hijacked our revolution and allowed the spread of political chaos, a growing economic crisis and religious strife. They also engage in extreme violence and torture towards peaceful protesters, as well as kill many in attacks. The military rulers of Egypt today are as untouchable as Mubarak and his cronies were for the past 30 years and until that changes, our struggle has yet to succeed.

We will continue to fight for our freedom until we can no longer stand.

FATMA GHALY: On Friday morning it looked like there were millions out on the streets. And I remember it was different: people were so fed up and they were not out only in Tahrir Square, they were out on the streets, in front of the parliament building, everywhere. People were charged and angry. They had expected so much and the speech was such an anti-climax. And I think at that point, the army must have decided, you know what? He can't do that to people.

We received another message that there would be a speech from the presidential palace, so we ran to a place where we could see a television. The vice-president came out for his famous 45-second speech that Mubarak was stepping down. I can't tell you what happened in Egypt that day. It was just so emotional. I can't believe it happened. I mean, *it happened!* No one believed that it would. But it did and Mubarak left. And I think people felt that they got their country back. Egypt was ours again.

Now there are possibilities. Now there is potential. If we

work for this country, things will come out of it. We can take this country to a really great place and give it what it deserves. It did not deserve all this; it did not deserve to suffer that way.

ATIF HUSSEIN: When Mubarak eventually stepped down, I was pleased but have since wondered what I was pleased about. My involvement in this whole revolution was driven by my principles and by my feeling as one with the Egyptians as a Muslim. With the nationalism that emerged from it, I couldn't help but wonder why my friends and I risked our lives.

I find myself contemplating the concept of identity once again. Wherever I lay my head is home, but I have yet to feel fully welcome here. As a Muslim I have always considered all Muslim land and people as one, and myself as being a part of them. But nationalism has once again divided us. To me it is a primitive concept. Countries have simply replaced tribes and the whole world operates under one big tribal system. Allegiances are forced upon us. We are all made to stand with our passports, flags and national anthems.

What makes someone an Egyptian? What gives someone the right to comment on Egyptian politics and have a say in it? What are Egyptian values? Is Egypt for Egyptians, with everyone else a possible enemy of the state? Values—and knowing what's right or wrong—no longer dictate action in this primitive world order.

As a teacher and educator, I strive to build independent thinking in my pupils. I try and instil values within them, and encourage them to differentiate between right and wrong based on human principles and not tradition. I hope the new Egypt will do the same.

SALAH EL-SHAMY: Of course now, I must say they have to calm down. These kids—and that is what they are, just a bunch of kids—achieved some great things. Now they need to go home and let people get back to work.

It is enough what they have done so far; but the future is not looking bright. It is very scary. The future will be scary unless the country gets back on track.

NAJAH NADI: We had gathered for the sunset prayer in front of the palace. After we finished, we heard that Mubarak had stepped down. We could not believe it. We kept asking if it was really true, and we celebrated and laughed with delight. We had joy in our hearts and our minds were at peace. We had gained a voice.

MAGED ABDEL WADOOD: The day [former vice-president] Omar Suleiman announced the president was leaving, I was really sad. I knew we would be left with chaos for a long time. We are good people, but there are a lot of bad people among us as well. On top of that, we have high levels of illiteracy and ignorance, and I worry we will not be able to manage things. Without a strong leader, we will have chaos.

My problem now is that the youth have no plan to fix the country. If they had a program and even 60 per cent of it made sense, I would have supported them. But they wanted to protest without having a clue what to do afterwards.

What are we doing putting all the businesspeople in jail, like common criminals? Some of these people employ thousands of Egyptians. It's like jailing the economy.

RASHA RAGHEB: I disliked Mubarak for several reasons: no political freedoms, corruption, poor education, no healthcare, terrible distribution of wealth, and many more. But I am shocked at how rude and disrespectful we Egyptians have become. No matter what Mubarak has done, there is no excuse for us to lift our shoes to his picture. We are a cultured and respectful people. In a way it is ironic that he is reaping what he has sown; he corrupted education and this is how the uneducated react, he starved people and this is how the hungry react. But we should have been better behaved. He should have been judged fairly and respectfully. This is a man who one day went to war for me and my country. He put his life at risk for me and my country. We should respect that.

AMR ABDULLAH: In January of 2011, I was in Syria, and I came back saying I wished the people in Egypt were more like the Syrians—how cultured, how clean, how aware, how much they care about beauty, so that even the cheapest sandwich is presented beautifully and the man making that sandwich is dressed cleanly and has a smile on his face. There, you could walk on the sidewalk for half a kilometer without tripping, whereas in Cairo you might trip every 10 meters. My point was that we had reached such a terrible state of deterioration in every aspect of life here. We now have to work in stages—we will need several phases to get us out of the pits we have reached.

IMAGES OF
THE REVOLUTION

Zeyad Gohary

ZEYAD GOHARY, 24, WORKS AS A FINANCIAL ANALYST IN CAIRO.
PHOTOGRAPHY IS HIS PASSION AND HE ENJOYS COVERING A
WIDE RANGE OF THEMES. HE COMES FROM A PRIVILEGED
BACKGROUND AND, LIKE MANY OTHER EGYPTIANS, HAD
NEVER PERCEIVED HIMSELF AS PARTICULARLY POLITICIZED
OR PATRIOTIC. BUT THE FERVOR OF THOSE 18 DAYS CHANGED
THAT. NOW, HE SAYS, HE IS A PROUD FLAG BEARER. HERE ARE
SOME OF THE IMAGES HE CAPTURED IN THE COURSE OF THOSE
PIVOTAL DAYS.

THE PROTESTS PROVIDED MANY CHALLENGES FROM A
TECHNICAL PERSPECTIVE. MR. GOHARY WAS KEEN TO KEEP HIS
EQUIPMENT LIGHT, IN CASE HE NEEDED TO RUN. HE ALSO HAD
TO MAKE THE DECISION TO BE AN OBSERVER AND PHOTOGRAPH
THE OTHERS, RATHER THAN BE AN ACTIVE DEMONSTRATOR. HE
USED HIS FASTEST LENS, THE NIKON 50MM F/1.8 PRIME LENS,
WHICH IS LIGHT, COMPACT AND PRODUCES IMAGES THAT ARE
VERY DEFINED. BUT IT MEANT THAT HE HAD TO BE CLOSE TO THE
ACTION. THE FEELING OF PROXIMITY IN THE PHOTOGRAPHS IS
REAL.

ARMED WITH HIS TRUSTY NIKON D90, MR. GOHARY ALSO
SHOT HIGH-QUALITY VIDEO, INCLUDING OF THE RIOT-
POLICE TRUCKS AS THEY PLOUGHED THROUGH THE HORDES
OF PEACEFUL PROTESTERS ON QASR EL-NIL BRIDGE, AND OF
PROTESTERS HUGGING RIOT-POLICE OFFICERS WHO HAD ONLY
JUST STOPPED FIRING TEAR GAS THEIR WAY.

SELMEYA

Protesters were penned densely in front of riot police on Qasr el-Nil Bridge. This photo was taken after people had stopped for prayer, during which the police fired water cannons on them. Prayers done, the people rose and start clapping and shouting, "Selmeya!" (Peaceful) and marching forward. Here, a riot policeman was preparing to fire tear gas at the already drenched protesters. We soon discovered that the water was sprayed to increase the painful effects of tear gas in the eyes and sinuses. —*Zeyad Gohary*

FIRST SIGN OF WHAT WAS TO COME

As Friday prayers took place, a wall of riot police armed with canes and shields emerged, standing shoulder to shoulder and completely surrounding the mosque and its immediate vicinity. We sensed they did not know what was expected of them. —*Zeyad Gohary*

THE FIRST OFFENCE

When we passed the Cairo Sheraton in Dokki Square, on our way to Tahrir, it was clear the riot police did not intend the day to proceed peacefully. Tear gas canisters fell out of the sky like a dirty hailstorm. Shortly after this photo was taken, a canister landed on the balcony of an apartment to the left of the frame. The apartment caught fire but the fire brigade was too busy hosing down protesters elsewhere to put that fire out. —*Zeyad Gohary*

THE PEOPLE DEMAND

As we marched past buildings, everyone began pleading to the supporters and onlookers to join the effort with chants of "INZIL!" or step down. —*Zeyad Gohary*

STOCK STILL

Security guards posted at the Dokki Police Station (to the right of the frame) were not part of the riot police but had a duty to protect the station. They did not leave even as everyone else fled from the effects of tear gas. I took cover behind them when the canister storm was at it fiercest. These men deserve to be honored. —*Zeyad Gohary*

DUTY AND SORROW

This riot police officer was crying as a result of having to fight his brothers and sisters. These men were devastated, but forced to follow orders or face serious consequences. As we walked past them, after they had ceased firing at us, a protester went up to them and told them they were forgiven. He hugged and kissed them and gave them water. Everyone knew who was to blame for the atrocities, and these poor policemen were not to blame. —*Zeyad Cohary*

EGYPT, YOUR SONS ARE MEN

I hope this photograph reaches as many people as possible so they can see and be reminded of the acts of bravery that took place on that day, like that of this man. —*Zeyad Gohary*

CHANGE

This homeless man did not move as he watched nearly 30,000 protesters march in front of him chanting against an oppressive regime and singing the national anthem. His only reaction was to cross his legs and watch, a perfect representation of Egypt before the revolt: an apathetic, sedated nation incapable of change. —*Zeyad Gohary*

REKINDLED PRIDE

As we walked through Zamalek district chanting our national anthem, this old man began to conduct us with his hat and cane, the force of his emotion apparent. He must have lived through WWII and Egypt's two wars with Israel, and since then Egypt had not had a reason to sing its anthem with such power and pride. I believe he suddenly remembered what it was like to fight for Egypt. —*Zeyad Gohary*

AND THEN THERE WAS JOY

Eighteen days of tension ended on February 11 with the fall of Hosni Mubarak. In true Egyptian fashion, people took to the streets. Unfortunately, I was not in Tahrir on that day, something I will always regret, but being with my family and celebrating in Heliopolis' historic Korba area was an experience I will never forget. —*Zeyad Gohary*

IN HIGH ESTEEM

I walked around Tahrir on the morning of February 12th. There were smiles on everyone's faces, national songs blasting from every direction, small groups of people happily chanting "The People Have Finally Deposed the Regime!" and a general sense of family among the thousands in the square. At that moment, the army was held on a pedestal so high you could say they were almost revered. —*Zeyad Gohary*

GOOD MORNING, CAIRO

Amid the excitement and national pride, it was time to put that enthusiasm into cleaning up. Roads were swept, and in some cases washed, pavements were re-painted, rubbish was transported to pre-arranged collection points, traffic remained largely organized by volunteers. I could not have imagined a better way to welcome our freshly awakened country than with this sincere act of ownership and teamwork. —*Zeyad Gohary*

WE NEVER LOST
OUR SENSE OF HUMOR

Although Egyptians had not been smiling for a couple of decades (there was precious little to smile about), they never stopped laughing. Political jokes have been a staple of Egyptian society for generations, albeit told in whispers. This revolution was no different, but the tellers were more vocal. The following jokes circulated before, during and after the revolution.

Humor Before the Revolution:

• Angel of death Azrael visits Hosni Mubarak to take his soul and advises him to say his goodbyes to the Egyptian people, to which Hosni responds:, "Why, where are they going?"

• Mubarak is taking a walk in the desert when he finds a large statue. He calls State Security and demands to find out who the statue is of. Ten minutes later, they call back and say it is a statue of Ramses the Third. "How did you find out?" he asks. State Security's answer: the statue confessed.

• Michael Jordan is going through airport security, but can't find his passport. The man at the gate asks him to prove he is Michael Jordan, so Jordan blindfolds himself and shoots 10 straight balls through the hoop. The security guard lets him in. Next comes Muhammad Ali, also without a passport. Put through the same test for identification, Ali proceeds to knock out all the people in the hall, and he too is allowed to pass. Then Hosni Mubarak comes to the gate, without his passport. The security guard asks him to do something to prove his identity. Hosni replies, "I don't know how to do anything." The security guard lets him through.

• [On Gamal Mubarak's involvement in most of Egypt's major business deals] A man enters a coffee shop and sees three portraits on the wall of Nasser, Sadat and Mubarak. He asks the owner who they are and the owner replies: "That is Nasser, the man who built the Aswan Dam, kicked the English out and freed Egypt from occupation. And that is Sadat, the great warrior who demolished the Israelis in 1973 and regained the Sinai Peninsula. And that third guy is the father of Gamal, co-owner of this coffee shop."
Humor During the Revolution:

• Breaking news: On hearing that Mubarak, if ousted, may run for office in Tunisia, Tunisians are organising demonstrations demanding ex-president Ben Ali's immediate return.

• Alaa Mubarak to Gamal Mubarak: "You know what Dad's biggest mistake was? He sold off the whole country but forgot to sell Tahrir Square."

• One stoner to another: "What is this Facebook?" The other guy replies: "Not sure exactly, but it helps remove presidents."
• Oxford dictionary: *Mubarak (v.),* to stick very effectively one thing to another, usually a throne or seat of power. As in, I will Mubarak you to that Senate Chair and you will never be removed. *Ghaddafi (adj.),* to be completely and utterly insane. Don't go ghaddafi on me, man, I know you have a brain.
• State Security announced today that they have identified the small group of dissidents who have started the revolution. There are around 80 million of them, and they use the code name "The Egyptian People".

• Father to Internet-addicted son: "If you don't do your homework, I will switch the Internet off." Son to dad: "Don't do it—you know what happened to the last guy who tried that, don't you?"

• During the complete absence of policemen on the street, this bumper sticker appeared: "To the police force that has abandoned the streets: Please come back, I am a thief and there's just no thrill in my work without you guys chasing."

• We have never had secular segregation in Egypt—we despise Ahmed Ezz [corrupt Muslim businessman] and Youssef Boutros [corrupt Christian Minister of Finance] equally!

• A man finds a magic lamp and rubs it. A genie comes out, steals the man's watch, and goes back in. The man rubs the lamp again, and the genie reappears. The man asks: "Why are you stealing my watch? Isn't this Alaa-din's lamp?", and the genie replies: "No, it is Alaa Mubarak's lamp."

• Hosni Mubarak addressing protesters leaving Tahrir Square after VP Omar Suleiman's speech announcing Mubarak's departure: "Hey, come back! Omar was just joking."

• On Channel 1 state television news: "The government denies the existence of the Ministry of Interior and advises all citizens not to be misled by the lies spread by various foreign sources about the existence of such a ministry."

• [During the complete lack of police presence on the streets] Suggested Mother's Day gifts for this year: Self-defence spray, electric Taser, one year's subscription for kung fu classes.

• First, the police slogan was: "Police in the Service of the People", then it became: "The Police and the People in the Service of the Country". Now it's: "Help Yourself!"

• After Mubarak's speech, Egyptian television threatens demonstrators that if they don't go home, they will repeat the speech endlessly.

• Bahraini demonstrators are requesting a support group of 900,000 Egyptians. They want to have a million-man march, but their population is only 100,000.

• Two men meet in Tahrir Square. One man says: "Terrorists have abducted Hosni Mubarak and are threatening to douse him in gasoline and burn him alive unless we give them US$5 million, so we're collecting donations." The second man says, "How much is the average donation?" The first man replies: "Five gallons."

• Constitution Article 202: In the unlikely case that the president dies suddenly, a Ouija board will be set up in a public area to communicate with him, and his soul shall rule the country until his oldest son takes over.

• Letter from an Egyptian student to the demonstrators: "Keep it short; we're going to have to study this soon!"

• Sign seen in Tahrir Square: "Please leave; we've run out of revolution jokes!"

Humor Post Revolution:

• Advertisement from Tahrir Square to all the Arab people: "Any president removed within 18 days, or your money back."

• For the first time in Egyptian history, dead people are not allowed to vote. Where is this democracy everyone is talking about? [It was a common practice to include dead voters in ballot counting during Mubarak's tenure.]

• Seen on a match-making website: "23-year-old, pretty, university educated, veiled girl, looking for intelligent, funny, average or better looking university graduate between 28 and 34. Must have Tahrir experience."

• State Security apologises for the loss of services in the last weeks and offers 15 days of free torture for every affected customer.

POEMS & SONGS
OF A REVOLUTION

*If, one day, a people desire to live, then fate will answer
their call.*

*And then their night will begin to fade, and their chains
to break and fall.*

*For he who is not embraced by a passion for life will
dissipate into thin air—*

*At least that is what all creation has told me, and what
its hidden spirits declare.*

"The Will of Life" is by the late Tunisian poet Abu al-Qasim al-Shabi, who has been renamed the poet of the Tunisian revolution. Professor Elliot Colla of Georgetown University, who translated the segment above, also describes al-Shabi as generally the poet of the Arab Spring.

While al-Shabi was Tunisian, Egypt's revolution also generated copious amounts of poetry—either poetry already penned by poets and used in previous revolutions, or clever, rhyming couplets in Arabic that became part of the slogans shouted in Tahrir Square and by people on the streets.

Al-Shabi died at a very young age in 1934, and yet his poem resounded with the revolutionaries of 2011. "It's a poem that any educated Arab would know," said Professor Colla. He explains that while an American or Briton might have trouble naming five or even three contemporary poets, and that poetry has long since been replaced by prose as a way of articulating modern events, within the Arab world poetry has never gone away.

"Poetry is the soundtrack of their life," he says. "In America, poetry is minor. In the Arab world, it's the opposite. It is a part of its education system. It's a living tradition that's more than 1,500 years old. There's a lot of material to draw on. If you're not educated, there's an extensive colloquial tradition to draw upon."

The Egyptian revolution of 2011 also witnessed the re-emergence of works stemming from the collaboration between poet Ahmed Fouad Negm, who had been actively writing poetry to enthuse revolutionaries and criticize the government since the 1970s, and musician Sheikh Imam. Many of Negm's poems were set to music by the late Imam. Around Tahrir Square, protesters, some of whom were too young to remember these two artists first time around, still found encouragement and courage from their poetry songs.

Professor Colla wrote in his article "The Poetry of Revolt" that this was not the first time that Egypt has had a revolution, and it was certainly not the first time poetry was used by the protesters. In 1881, there was the Urabi Revolution, which overthrew a corrupt royal family. The 1881 chosen poet was Mahmoud Sami al-Baroudi. The 1919 revolution nearly brought down British military rule, and at this time the colloquial poetry of Bayram al-Tunsi could be heard. And the 1952 revolution, which heralded the era of presidents Nasser, Sadat and Mubarak, played to the patriotic verse of celebrated singer Abdel Halim Hafez. It came as no surprise to Professor Colla that Negm's poetry should be used by the Tahrir revolutionaries. His poetry praises the courage of ordinary Egyptians and strongly criticizes the Egyptian government.

One of the current poets chosen by those in Tahrir was Tamim Barghouti, a Cairo-born Palestinian poet who is also a colleague of Professor Colla at Georgetown. In earlier interviews, Barghouti spoke about how touched he was to be contacted by those in Tahrir, and suddenly was reading out his poetry every two hours via video link to a huge screen in Tahrir Square. "Barghouti's poetry has a clear political agenda," says Professor Colla. "It's almost sermonesque."

But those in Tahrir Square were quick to add their own wit and flair to literary couplets that graced posters and were shouted by the tens of thousands taking part. They all had their own musical rhythms:

"Yâ Mubârak! Yâ Mubârak! Is-Sa'ûdiyya fi-ntizârak!," (Mubarak, O Mubarak, Saudi Arabia awaits!), with Saudi Arabia being in reference to the former president of Tunisia Ben Ali fleeing to Riyadh.

There was also: "Shurtat Masr, yâ shurtat Masr, intû ba'aytû kilâb al-'asr" (Egypt's Police, Egypt's Police, You've Become Nothing But Palace Dogs).

Poetry, songs and artistic works became a part of the 18 days in Tahrir. Sculptors turned the stones thrown at protesters into sculptures in the square. There were artists' corners where artwork and graffiti were displayed, and children could also paint and draw. Despite the violence, tear gas, bullets and water cannons, artists found a voice at Tahrir and it was not long before stages were erected for impromptu concerts, some from Egypt's well-known singers and poets, others simply by people with guitars and drums who entertained the crowds as they wandered around Tahrir.

Many well-known bands and singers entertained and uplifted the crowds in Tahrir. (There was also one who took the first plane out, and might have found that his career was subsequently affected by that move.) While some singers, poets and actors had always tried to be controversial and take a stab at the government, they were working under very difficult constraints, so some of the artistic and literary fields had suffered because of that. Former president Hosni Mubarak had appointed one culture minister, Farouk Hosni, for more than 20 years, which begs the question: just how much room for artistic growth was there? Artists, novelists and filmmakers faced stringent censorship, even from within Hosni's department. So here, finally, was a chance for those who had never had it, to express themselves. Flourishing songwriters emerged and, subsequent to the revolution, these past months have seen many novels, songs and poems spring from the inspiration of those heady days in Tahrir.

Perhaps the poster boy of Tahrir on the singing side was rap artist Rami Essam who, at just 23, inspired many within Tahrir, on Facebook and on YouTube, where many other bands also posted their revolutionary songs. Essam gained musical-hero status on the stage in Tahrir, but just a few months later was badly beaten by army soldiers, when he and others were arrested at a subsequent demonstration in Tahrir. There is some way to go before Egyptians will be allowed to fully express themselves.

International singers were also inspired to pen their own songs about the revolution. These included the American rock singer Jon Bon Jovi with his song "No Apologies", and Canadian teen idol Justin Bieber, who highlighted the revolution to a much younger generation worldwide with "Higher".

ACKNOWLEDGEMENTS

It is tradition to make a comprehensive list of people I wish to thank in this section. My list would have to include all the martyrs of our revolution who, as we go to print, have exceeded one thousand. The list would be prohibitively long.

Instead, I wish to thank my publisher Dania Shawwa Abuali, under whose vigilant eye this book came to fruition. My editorial advisor, Annemarie Evans, was a pleasure to work with: demanding yet supportive, critical yet complementing.

My wife, my children and my colleagues at work all suffered to one degree or another as I redirected my time away from them and towards this book.

All the contributors to this work are especially worthy of gratitude—they were generous with their time and, perhaps more importantly, their feelings and memories of those unrivalled eighteen days in Tahrir.

Having failed to thank the martyrs by name, I owe it to their pure spirits, at the very least, to dedicate this book to them. May they rest in peace, in a place far better than the world we live in.

—HR

HATEM RUSHDY, EDITOR

Cairo businessman Hatem Rushdy interrupted his normal life on January 25th, 2011, to join the mass protests to oust President Hosni Mubarak. He attended the protests in Tahrir Square every day for 18 days. His access to protesters on the ground, and his decision to collect and preserve their stories in detail during those heady days, lead to this book being born.

Mr. Rushdy runs People Plus, an executive search firm in Cairo. Born in Egypt in 1968, he grew up in Kuwait before returning to study at the American University in Cairo. He holds an MSc from the University of Manchester in the UK. He was previously a headhunter at KPMG Egypt, and Vodaphone's youngest director. He has written children's stories and extensive articles on business and tourism. Mr. Rushdy is married with three children, and is preparing to play an active role in Egypt's unfolding political scene.

AHDAF SOUEIF

Ahdaf Soueif is the author of the bestselling *The Map of Love*, which was shortlisted for the Booker Prize for Fiction in 1999. Ms. Soueif is also a political and cultural commentator. A collection of her essays, *Mezzaterra: Fragments from the Common Ground*, was published in 2004. Her translation (from Arabic into English) of Mourid Barghouti's *I Saw Ramallah* also came out in 2004. She lives with her children in London and Cairo.

ANNEMARIE EVANS

Annemarie Evans is a British broadcast and print journalist based in Hong Kong, where she has lived for nearly two decades. She works for the BBC World Service in addition to Radio Television Hong Kong, where she sometimes co-hosts the evening news programme and also has her own weekly programme. She previously worked for the foreign desk of the *South China Morning Post* and has a keen interest in current affairs both in Asia and the Middle East. Annemarie Evans was the editorial advisor for *18 Days in Tahrir*.